MW01245300

MARY
IN THE
BIBLE
WORTHY MOTHER OF SALVATION

GREGMARY EMEKA AJIDE

XULON PRESS

MARY IN THE BIBLE
WORTHY MOTHER OF SALVATION

A TREASURE FOR CATHOLICS AND A PRECIOUS GIFT FOR NON-CATHOLICS

GREG-MARY EMEKA AJIDE

(Unworthy Servant of Jesus and Mary)

Nihil Obstat: Very Rev. Msgr. Dr. Jerome Madueke
Censor Deputatus, Diocese of Awka
22nd March, 2001.

imprimatur: **Most Rev. Dr. Simon A. Okafor**
Catholic Bishop of Awka
22nd March, 2001.

Xulon Press
2301 Lucien Way #415
Maitland, FL 32751
407.339.4217
www.xulonpress.com

1st Published: 2001

Revised Edition: 2009

Printed in the United States of America.

ISBN-13: 9781545622100

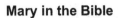

"In these predestined times the increased efforts of the forces of evil can only be countered by a corresponding increase of devotion to the Most Blessed Virgin Mary".

"*Satan is the greatest enemy of our salvation. He is the one engaged in battle with the Virgin Mary; he will therefore attack this work with all his armoury ; even making use of some Catholics but in the end the Immaculate Heart of Mary will triumph*".

Author's prophecy

DEDICATION

The Blessed Virgin says: *"You love Me and make others love Me."* This book is dedicated to thee, Dear Queen and Gate of Heaven, as an Act of love to honour Thine Immaculate Conception, Divine Maternity and Glorious Assumption. It is also dedicated to Thee, O Merciful Mother on behalf of the soul of my brother, Rev. Fr. Godfrey Nwankwo, who was murdered three months after his ordination by unknown assassins, my late father, Joseph Ajide, the aborted babies, the motherless, the unbaptized, the lukewarm Catholics, the gone-astray, as well as in reparation for my sins, the sins of my family, and those of the whole world.

TO THE READER

For proper understanding of this book, please, say these prayers.

"Come Holy Spirit; come by means of the powerful intercession of the Immaculate Heart of Mary, your well-beloved Spouse". (Once).

"Jesus, Mary, I love You, save souls," Amen. (3times)

"My dear friends of God, it is better to offend Jesus (though you should not do this) than to offend his mother Mary. The reason is that if you offend Jesus, Mary will plead for your pardon. But if you offend the Virgin Mary, your intercessor, tell me, who will plead for you?" Who will intercede for you?"

AUTHOR'S PRAYER TO THE BLESSED VIRGIN

Hail Mary, White Lily of the Glorious and always serene Trinity. Hail brilliant Rose of the Garden of heavenly delights: O You, by whom God wanted to be born and by whose milk the King of heaven wanted to be nourished! Nourish the souls of all persons who shall read this book with effusions of divine grace, that they may come to the knowledge of their heavenly Mother so as to come to the better knowledge of the Divine Master, Christ Jesus. O my Jesus, please, give me your heart because I want to love your Blessed Mother Mary as You have loved Her. O Mary, if all creatures could know You. O, who could love You as You truly deserve! I console myself when I remember that many saintly souls in heaven and upon earth are enamoured of your loveliness and goodness. Above all, I rejoice when I remember that God Himself loves you more than all men and angels put together. O my beloved Queen, even I, a wretched sinner, love You. However, I love You too little. O perfect Moulder, please, mould me as You have moulded your Son Jesus: for I long for a more intense and more tender love for You. To love You is a sure sign of predestination and a grace that God grants to those that are saved. O Mother of Jesus and my merciful and powerful Mother, reject not my prayers in my necessities, but join to them your very own prayers so that in You, with You, through You, by You, and for You, I may glorify the Most Blessed Trinity God the Father who gave You to us, God the Son who showed You to us, and God the Holy Spirit who showed You the light, for all eternity, O Clement, O Loving, O Sweet Virgin Mary, amen.

WHAT THE PROTESTANTS SAY ABOUT THIS BOOK

1.This book is wonderfully inspired by God and his Blessed Mother. It is full of facts about Virgin Mary in the Bible. It has greatly enlightened and enabled me realize that Mary is indispensable in the work of salvation. In fact, I have come to realize that all persons who aspire to meet Jesus at the end of their earthly life must begin to do so now through Mary else ... However, whoever is in doubt of what I have just said should very quickly pick a copy of 'Mary in the Bible' and he will find the truth. Today, I use it to teach, dialogue with, and correct my fellow pastors in the pentecostal, anglican, protestant, and other non-Catholic denominations.

> **Pastor Paul Aduaka**
> *Holy Sabbath Mission*
> *Ifitedunu, Anambra State.*

2.Although I am an Anglican woman, my encounter with Greg-Mary and his book- 'Mary in the Bible' has brought light into my life. The book explains in details the indispensable role of Mary in the salvation of man, with references to Biblical quotations. In all truth, this young man is full of divine inspirations. With this wonderful publication I have discovered that Catholics read and live the Bible, whereas other Christians merely read it.

> **Anonymous From Ogidi,**
> *Idemili Local Gov't,*
> *Anambra State.*

3. Although I am a protestant by birth, I must confess that since the visit of Greg-Mary to our school, I have learned from his talks, and especially from his book *'Mary In The Bible'*, the vital role of the Virgin Mary in the salvation of man. I got myself consecrated to the Immaculate Heart of Mary when Greg-Mary organized consecration for the school. Today, I wear my scapular, recite my holy rosary and go to mass etc.

Anonymous
Girls' Sec. School,
Umudioka, Anambra State.

4. I thank God and his Blessed Mother, Mary, for this precious gift *'Mary in the Bible'*, given to mankind through Greg-Mary, their chosen instrument. Although I have always acknowledged Mary's exceptional holiness, as an arch-Anglican, I have never had any special devotion to her. But after reading through this heavenly inspired publication, I realized I was ignorant of the Bible, with regards to Virgin Mary's position in the salvation of man. Truly, she is indispensable in this noble task. This book has become my daily spiritual reading. Today, I practice true devotion to Mary, and I pray that my fellow Protestants should follow suit.

Sis. L.O. Ogechukwu
St. Paul's Anglican Church,
Box 25, Ikenga-Ogidi,
Anambra State.

WHAT THE CATHOLIC PRIESTS SAY ABOUT THIS BOOK

1. Having gone through this piece, I stand to testify the devotedness of the author which is beyond mere academic exercise. It is indeed a library of Mariology that educates the ignorant, encourages the lukewarm, stabilizes the fanatics and assures the faithful of a fulfilled end. Every family should use it as its daily spiritual book.
Rev. Fr. Donatus Ezenneka

2. This book is both edifying and enlightening. I see it not just a work of the human mind, but of a mind inspired by the Holy Spirit and guided by the love of God. The author has taken great pains to search through the scriptures and traditions of the church to highlight, in very clear terms, the indispensable role of the Blessed Virgin Mary in the work of salvation. I recommend it to all Catholics for their edification, and to all non-Catholics for their enlightenment.
Very Rev. Fr. Dr. Clemence Uche

3. A writer is dear and necessary for us only in the measure in which he reveals to us the truth and facts about life. Greg-Mary has in this simple work enriched our knowledge of the Blessed Virgin Mary. This work remains a rare source. For Catholics, it leads them on, but for non-Catholics, especially the unreasonable critics of our dear Mother Mary, it remains a source of light to the truth. Read on.
Very Rev. Fr. Bede Moore Udechukwu

4. This publication is quite enriching and educative. I pray that all will comply with it.

Very Rev. Fr. Dr. Alex Nwachukwu

5.This booklet is a book for the time. I very sincerely recommend it to all. It will inform the uninformed, direct the misinformed, guide and strengthen the believer in faith.
Rev. Fr. Chike E. Ubah

6.This booklet answers some of the questions some uninformed Christians and non- Christians ask about Mary and Marian devotions. I recommend it for publication.
Very Rev. Fr. Martin O. Madueke

7.Greg-Mary has written this book from the depth of his experience as a Marian enthusiast. This reflection is interesting, simple, and good for public consumption. I warmly recommend it to every Christian who wishes to know more about Virgin Mary.
Rev. Fr. Charles Ugwu

8. The book *'Mary in the Bible'* written by Greg-Mary, is a singular and a welcome advancement in the Catholic Church, for a proof of Mary Mother of God, as the Mother of humanity, Mediatrix of all graces and Co-redemptrix. I therefore, recommend it to all and sundry. Thanks a lot.
Very Rev. Fr. Frank Oranefo

9.This book was given to me by a friend as a gift, in Austria. Having gone through it, and also heard the author speak when I traveled to Nigeria, I stand to testify that it is the glory of Jerusalem and a great light to the Gentiles.

Very Rev. Fr. C. Ezekwugo
Founder, Opus Angelorum.

ACKNOWLEDGMENTS

At the completion of this work, I wish to thank the Most Blessed Trinity to whom I appealed daily and nightly while this writing took place. In every undertaking we are called to offer praises and thanksgiving to God. He is worthy to receive glory and honour, power and might, wisdom and thanksgiving, for He made creation for his own and for the salvation of humankind. Without God's love, mercy and grace, this work would not have been possible. All through the reading, studying and writing of this book: *"Mary in the Bible"*, He empowered me with his efficacious grace. I therefore, prostrate before Him, in truthful adoration and thanksgiving.

My filial love and gratitude go to Our Most Blessed Mother and Sovereign Mistress - the Divine Mary, whose unceasing prayers and glorious intercession, protection, counselling, generosity and inspiration facilitated this exercise.

I am particularly grateful to the Holy Father, Pope John Paul II. His teachings and devotion to Mary encouraged me greatly. I thank, in a special way, His Lordship, Most Rev. Dr. Simon A. Okafor, the Catholic Bishop of Awka whose *Imprimatur* gives adequate credibility to this publication. My profound gratitude goes to Very Rev. Monsignor Dr. Jerome Madueke, the Censor Deputatus, Catholic Diocese of Awka. He censored this book, advised me, wrote foreword one, and gave his *Nihil Obstat*. I am ever grateful to my peace making parish priest, Very Rev. Fr. Martin Madueke, and his humble assistant, Rev. Fr. Charles Ugwu. Their advice to me and devotion to Our Heavenly Empress helped me tremendously. I am also not forgetting my beloved friend, Rev. Fr.

Bede Moore Udechukwu. He encouraged me to pray more to Mary, to help me in the pursuit of this book.

I am truly indebted to the following Priests for the unspeakable spiritual assistance they gave me: Very Rev. Monsignor Dr. B.K. Nwazojie, Very Rev. Msgr. Prof. Festus Okafor, Rev. Fr. Ernest Simple Okoli, Rev. Fr. Val Mgbemena, Rev. Fr. Ignatius Onwuatuegwu, Rev. Fr. Paul Azuako, Very Rev. Fr. Cyril Nwizugbo (Late), Rev. Fr. Frank Oranefo, Rev. Fr. Martin Anusi, Rev. Fr. Francis Nwachukwu, and Rev. Fr. John Bosco Oghadugha.

My special thanks go to Chief Dr. A. B. C. Nworah, Chief Barr. Emma Okonkwo, Chief Barr. I.I. Ekwerekwu, Daddy Stephen Iloduba, Mrs. Eucharia Okpara, Mr. Nathanael Okongwu, Mr. Vicent De Paul Mobi, Miss Regina Onwuli, Mrs. Victoria Nwosu and family, Mrs. Virginia Asomugha and family, Mr. and Mrs. George Eneh, and Mrs. Mary Oruche of the Blessed Sacrament. All these people supported me in various capacities.

My most profound love goes to my beloved Mum, Mrs. Virginia Erusaku Ajide, my brothers and sisters, my beloved wife, Benedicta Ajide, my relations, my friends and well wishers. May the Lord God bless you all, and may the Blessed Virgin Mary watch over you!

FOREWORD ONE

This book, Mary In The Bible, written by Greg-Mary Emeka Ajide, treats some questions people ask concerning the mystery of Mary and devotions attached to her such as the Rosary, the Scapular, the Angelus and the Litany. Here, the author responds in a personal way to the challenges of St. Paul who urges Christians to have a defence ready when questioned about the foundation of their faith.

Fundamentalism and Pentecostalism will continue to launch its insidious attack on the Roman Catholic Church. With the geometric spread of sects in recent years, and their greater use of modern means of social communications, this attack increases daily in ferocity, intent on dealing some blows on every bastion of Catholic belief.

These attacks not withstanding, the Church is evermore determined to uphold and propagate her age-old teachings. These times are being described as the age of Mary, when Marian devotees are counting in millions round the world. News of Marian apparitions punctuate the air, as new shrines are consecrated in her honour. Catholics are being summoned not only to cherish the teachings about Mary and nourish their piety, but to seek out new methods and expressions to present the Mystery of Mary to the present generation (cf. Paul VI, Evengelii Nuntiandi, n. 3).

This booklet, *Mary in the Bible*, is an attempt to offer apologetics on some articles of faith that are often touched upon in contemporary debates. Copious biblical citations are adduced to establish the foundations of the truths of faith selected. Some students of modern Biblical scholarship might accuse the author of being sometimes unrestrained in his accommodation. But if the use of allegory is still legitimate as a method in biblical studies, the author is warranted to seek the spiritual sense of passages he cited. The historic figures cited are hence given deeper significance in this booklet. The details and characters of these historic figures are utilized to uncover the hidden mystery of the Blessed Virgin Mary which the author believes is contained in the biblical passages.

When one considers the preposterous arguments advanced by the fundamentalists and Pentecostals to dislodge Catholics of the foundations of their apostolic faith, popular biblical references such as offered in this booklet become desirable. It was St. Hilary (d.367) who once said:

"The errors of heretics and blasphemers force us to deal with unlawful matters, to scale perilous heights, to speak unutterable words, to trespass on forbidden ground. Faith ought in silence to fulfill the commandments, worshipping the Father, reverencing with him the Son, abounding in the Holy Spirit, but we must strain the poor resources of our languages to express thoughts too great for words. The error of others compels us to err in daring to embody in human terms truths which ought to be hidden in the silent veneration of the heart" (De Trinitate, 2.2).

About the theology of Mary, the Second Vatican Council (1963-1965) has opened new perspectives that are biblical, ecclesiological and ecumenical. Current post-conciliar documents go further to urge for an anthropological approach which considers Mary as the prophetic woman of contemporary struggles for liberation. Mary not only announced the liberation of the poor from the historical social injustices of her time, she remains the hope for the hungry and the down trodden of the present world. For this reason, some protestant feminists have begun to lay down their arms and to cultivate devotion to Mary, the Mother of God.

Greg-Mary has thoroughly researched on the treasures of the Bible and the spiritual writings of some Church's acclaimed Marian devotees of the past. The trend of his arguments followed closely those of St. Louis Marie De Montfort whom he often cited. Using the method of spiritual exegesis of the earliest patristic era, he set himself to examine some Old and New Testament quotations which support the Catholic teachings on Mary and other related subjects like scapular, medal, rosary, litany etc.

Greg-Mary Emeka Ajide did not hide his affection for the Blessed Virgin Mary. I was particularly enriched, reading through his work. About the mystery of Mary, he demonstrates again the ancient adage that one cannot say enough. The much he has said here, it is my prayer, should be able to inspire and sustain many Marian devotees and persuade some doubting Thomases.

Very Rev. Msgr. Dr. Jerome Madueke
Director, Fides Communications,
Catholic Diocese of Awka,
Okpuno, Anambra State.

FOREWORD TWO

It is not often that I have read any book that captivated me as Greg
Mary Ajide's Mary In The Bible. Yet Greg Mary is neither a priest,
nor a theologian, nor a philosopher. Where then did he get all the
knowledge in spirituality, all the insight manifested, all the
eloquence exhibited? Then, I remembered sweet Jesus saying in
Mtt. 11:25, *"I thank you, Father, Lord of heaven and earth, because you
have shown to the unlearned what you have hidden from the wise and
learned"*.

Obviously, Mary In The Bible is a book full of inspiration, written
in fluent, simple, intelligible language. Right from the beginning,
the author's use of the Douay Version text of the Bible to portray
the intention of God in *Gen. 3: 15*, to the effect that SHE (not He or
IT) will crush the head of the mortal enemy of man (the serpent),
is most appropriate and serves as a most genuine kick off point.
His explanation (in page 7) of God's mysterious language in *Jer. 31:
22* with regard to a woman compassing a man is very insightful.

The author's explanation (in page 26: Jesus shows us the woman)
as to why Jesus addressed Mary as *"Woman"*, instead of *"Mother"*,
is profound and sublime. In brief, Christ acted accordingly so as to
identify Mary as the Woman of promise and the Woman of
prophecy who, together with her Son, would bring God's glory to
man.

Chapter 6 which portrays the fact that *"Only Jesus is born of Mary"*
and the usage of *Ezk. 44: 2-3* to buttress that fact, as well as the
revealing information in that section with regard to the relatives
of Jesus and Mary, is a delightful manifestation of insightful

scholarship. Another very insightful section is page 134 - *"Channel of Fulfilled Promises"*.

The section on the Rosary is very good and conveys excellent insight. Furthermore, the connection of *Ps 45: 17 with Lk. 1: 48,* is inspirational. Indeed, the Magnificat of Mary has become the song that will make her name remembered forever. As a matter of fact, it is said or song every day by the ordained ministers of the Catholic Church, among others, throughout the world.

The book's views regarding *Song of Songs 6: 10* (Chapter 8) which the legionaries of Mary use for their daily invocation, portrays veritable scholarship, especially where the author brought St. Alphonsus De Liguori to bear on the latter.

With regard to the section about *"Worshipping"* Mary, I am glad that the author is in agreement with my exposition on the matter in my book: *Honouring or Worshipping Mary*.

It may be necessary to mention that although some of the Biblical quotations used in the book can be applied to other situations appropriately, they also do make sense when applied to Mary.

On the whole, what comes out very vividly in reading the book, is what I consider the profound truth about devotion to Mary, namely, the Roman Catholic Church is doing the will of God by honouring Mary, whether in terms of the recitation of the *Hail Mary* (the *Ave Maria),* or in terms of the recitation of the *Rosary* and other Marian Prayers. Consequently, whoever decides not to honour Mary is deciding not to do the will of God and will face the consequences of such decision.

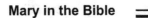

I acclaim the author of this book, and I do recommend the book, *Mary In The Bible,* to everyone on God's earth.

Very Rev. Msgr. Prof. Festus C. Okafor,
Professor of Education,
University of Nigeria, Nsukka.

TABLE OF CONTENTS

INTRODUCTION

Accroding to the letter of Saint Paul to the Romans, chapter three, verse twenty three *(Rm. 3: 23)*, all men have sinned and fallen short of God's grace. This fall of man originated from the disobedience of Adam and Eve the very first parents of the human race. And it brought as punishment eternal death. But God in his infinite mercy decided to restore the fallen human race to life. In order to do this, it became necessary that he would make use of a second Adam Jesus Christ, and a second Eve - the Blessed Virgin Mary. Again, since Eve was the person that actually sinned and brought death upon the human race, the Most Holy Mary would become the portal of divine mercy and the instrument through which life would be given to the human race.

In spite of these facts, rooted in the Bible and clarified by the church's tradition, some Christians continue to turn away from the Virgin Mary. They argue that since Jesus is the Saviour of mankind, Mary's role in the economy of salvation is insignificant. With this argument, they separate the inseparables Jesus and Mary.

If you (the Reader) look into the world today, you will discover that two groups of people exist in the Christian family. There are people who believe that only Jesus is important in the work of salvation. There are other people who maintain that Jesus and Mary are jointly important in the work of salvation. It appears that these people are fighting each other every day over whose belief is right. It seems as if this problem has entered into heaven, such that Jesus and Mary also fight each other every day. When God called Jesus to know what actually the problem was, he said he does not want people to honour the Virgin Mary rather, all men should honour him all alone. He also said he would want to take everything that belonged to him, to honour and glorify him every day. So, God said to him: *"Son, take whatever thing that belongs to you"*. Jesus got up and took the whole world, the whole of heaven, and everything that was in them, including you and me, and there was nothing left for the holy Virgin to take. But when God asked Mary to look round and see if there was anything belonging to her, she confidently got up, moved straight - away to Jesus and took him by the hand and said: *"This is my son, this is my possession"*.

Children of God, have you not seen that as Mary carries Jesus along, so shall the whole world, the whole of heaven, and every other thing belonging to Jesus go along with her? This goes to show that Jesus and Mary are inseparably one. Whatever belongs to Jesus, instantly belongs to Mary, and vice versa. Thus, if Mary and Jesus are inseparable, it follows that Mary and God are inseparable because Jesus Christ himself is God - *Isaiah 9: 6; Jn. 20: 28.*

In a bid to draw people away from God and bring them into his own kingdom, especially in these predestined times when the wicked least deserve the mercy of God, Satan has continued to deceive the humankind by preventing them from entering into the wonderful, mysterious portal which God has opened for the just ones, through which they can find access to his mercy. Oh, he has continued to hold captive his victims by making them not to see, believe, receive and accept the wonderful light of God by which they can dispel the gloom that envelopes the eyes of their minds. This mysterious Portal of Mercy this wonderful Light of God this suitable Remedy, by which the heavenly Father plans to restore the fallen human race to his grace, is his Most Blessed Mother the Most Blessed Virgin Mary. This world has become so satanically possessed, devastated and religiously deranged. It is such that almost nobody seems to notice the danger which is posed to our salvation network *The True Devotion to Mary,* by Satan and his human agents the so called Bible believers the Biblicists - the Modernists and the New Generation Churches, with their wind swept question: *Where is Mary in the Bible?* The humankind has, as a result of this ungodly question, become so ignorantly, blindly, proudly, helplessly, hopelessly, foolishly, ungratefully and un-religiously biblical such that almost everyone is now becoming unrepentantly selective in the teachings and commandments of God.

What is now common among non-Catholic Christians, is selecting a portion of the Bible and misinterpreting it to suit their deceitful and blasphemous claims, thereby making it very difficult for the simple minds and the less educated to understand and appreciate the Bible, as intended by God. For example, very many of those self-appointed pastors, prophets and prophetesses whom we see every time (on the television screen, at crusade centres, on the streets and in moving buses, in the pages of newspapers and magazines, as well as on the radio waves), are basing most of their false teachings and beliefs solely on this portion of the Bible: *"I am the way, the truth, and the life, no one comes to the father except by me" Jn 14: 6.* It is as if any other means of true devotion to God which is not directly through Christ is idolatry. If I may ask, as we all know that Jesus is the way to his father in heaven, which way then are we to follow in order to reach Jesus Christ Himself? As we get set to answer this question, let us not fail to consider the fact that the *circle* of salvation revolves round God the Father, to the Angels, to God the Holy Spirit, to the Virgin Mary (Who is also a saint), to God the Son (Jesus Christ), and back to the Father. When any of these entities is removed, salvation equation becomes unbalanced. Have we forgotten that it is the same Jesus who maintains that he is the way to the Father that again tells us that man's eternal life is dependent on every word (not just some words) that God speaks *Mt. 4: 4?* And one of the things that God has spoken is thus: *"All generation must call Mary Blessed" Ps. 45: 17; Lk.1:48.* Another thing is the last *Will* and *Testament* of Jesus on earth with regard to Mary: *"Woman, behold your son, son, behold your mother" Jn. 19: 26 27.* With these facts, it seems to us that Jesus chooses to hide behind his mother whom he constantly presents to us to follow. Yes, because he wills that it should be the immaculate Mary who loves him in us. Again, because it was through the Virgin Mary that Jesus passed from heaven to earth, Mary is called the Gate of heaven. Therefore, while Jesus is the way to his Father in heaven, Mary is the way to Jesus Christ her Son. Jesus is God and no one other than his Blessed Mother can approach him directly because he moves in an unapproachable light *1 Tim. 6: 16*. Hence the reason why he constantly points the way to her.

It is not surprising that up till this time, Jesus Christ is still not known, loved, followed, appreciated, obeyed, adored and preached as he ought to be because Virgin Mary, the immaculate Channel through which he came into the world, is kept in the background and withheld from souls.

Today, you hear the same people who have bluntly refused to welcome the Most Blessed Virgin Mary, shouting on top of their voices, *"We have received Jesus"*. If I may ask, can a person who does not welcome the source of light be in possession of light? Jesus is light and Mary is the source. Can a person who does not welcome the Ark, be in possession of the content of the Ark? Answer these questions, yourself. But let me warn you, beware of the type of Jesus you claim to have received. There are so many Jesus in the world today, but the only Jesus who is Christ the one and the only Saviour, is that one born, nurtured, and offered on the cross for our salvation by the Most Blessed Virgin.

Many Christians have vowed never to welcome the Virgin

Mary into their life and have recourse to her as a means to go to Jesus, on the grounds that such practices and devotions are not found in the Bible. It is on account of this that I have picked up my poor pen, with total submission to the powerful and glorious intercession, grace, leadership, protection, counseling and inspiration of the Holy Worthy Mother of God, who is also my Mother, my Queen, my Life, my Salvation, my Mistress and my All, to write from the Bible and the teachings of the Church, the little I can, on the subject, Mary In The Bible or Marian Biblical Awareness. It is hoped that it will help everyone both Christians and non-Christians Israelites and Gentiles Catholics and non-Catholics, to have a good knowledge of this woman Most Blessed among women, so that we can have a better knowledge of Jesus Christ her Son, love him, follow him, appreciate him, adore him, obey him, and preach him to the whole world to know better.

Although it is certain that the knowledge and the kingdom of Jesus Christ must come into the world, it must come but through the knowledge and the kingdom of his Mother Mary. For Mary's kingdom is Christ's kingdom, and Christ's kingdom is Mary's kingdom *Ps. 45: 9.* And since it was she who brought him into the world for the first time, it will also be she who will make his second and royal coming full of glory and splendour. As God the Father willed to start and to complete his greatest works by Mary ever since He created her *Gen. 3: 15; Lk. 1: 26 38; Gal. 4: 4 5; Jn. 19: 25 30,* He will not change either in his sentiments or in his conduct. For He is

God and does not change *Mal. 3: 6; Heb. 13: 8.* The gift of God is irrevocable *Rm. 11:29.*

To know the Most Blessed Virgin is to know Jesus Christ, the fruit of her womb. In the explanation of Christ about the knowledge of the father, he says that no one knows the son except the father, and no one knows the father except the son and those to whom the son chooses to reveal him *Mt. 11: 27; Lk. 10: 22.* In the same way, no one knows the mother except the son, and no one knows the son except the mother and those to whom the mother chooses to reveal him. As Jesus reveals God to man, so does Virgin Mary reveal Jesus to man.

According to the book of *Hosea 4:6,* God says: *"Oh, my people are perishing because they do not know me".* Yes, children of God, lots of people are suffering and perishing everyday for lack of knowledge of God because they do not know the Virgin Mary the woman who brought restoration of life by giving mortal existence to immortal God. But God in his own wisdom made it impossible for people to know him by means of their own wisdom, instead, by means of the so-called *'foolish'* message which we preach about Jesus and Mary *1 Cor.1: 21.* The more we know and honour the divine Mary, the more perfectly we come to the knowledge and adoration of Jesus Christ her son and the lesser the problems we encounter in this life. The more we love and follow the Virgin Mary, the more perfectly we love and follow Jesus Christ and the easier we move into the kingdom of heaven.

This is because to love the most Blessed Virgin is a sure sign of predestination and a grace that God gives to those that are saved.

The mysteries of the life of the Virgin Mary are so great that no mind, human or angelic, can fully understand them. God's ways are not our ways and his thoughts are not our thoughts *Isaiah 55: 8*. The *'foolishness'* of God in making the Blessed Virgin what she is today, tomorrow, and forever, is greater than human wisdom *1cor.1:25*. The knowledge of God's own mother requires total humility, total dependence, and abandonment of oneself to the grace of God. Only the souls who are born in Jesus and Mary can understand what I am saying. God himself did not reveal these mysteries in the early church because the faithful at that time would not have understood them. This was the reason why Jesus Christ, the Son of God and Son of the Virgin Mary, said in *Jn. 16: 12-13* , *"I have much more to teach you, but now it would be too much for you to understand. When, however, the spirit comes, who reveals the truth about God, he will lead you into all the truth"*. And when you know the truth, it will set you free *Jn. 8:32*.

Children of God, do you really want to know the truth about Mary, as intended by God in the salvation of the human family? If you do, then, come and follow me to the Bible, and our journey shall take us from Genesis to Revelation, because the Blessed Virgin is also the Mother and the Queen of the *'Word'* of God. She alone is the Empress and Mistress of the Bible.

Come, my brother, come, my sister, come home. It is you that I am calling. Yes, it is you. Yes, you who ask, *"Where is Mary in the Bible?"* Please, humble yourself so that you may be able to learn those things which you do not know about Mary, as intended by God and hidden in the Bible. Emulate the Ethiopian Eunuch. He humbled himself and was taught by Philip those things which he did not know, which are in the Bible *Acts 8:26 39.*

Finally, this booklet whose sole aim is the salvation of the human family, offers answers to most of the controversial questions people ask about Mary and Marian devotions. Are there places in the Bible where she can be found to be necessary to both God and man? Does God approve praying to Mary, Angels and saints? Is she truly the mother of God? Is she the mother of the Christian family? Can the Most Holy Rosary be found in the Bible? What are the powers of the rosary? Answers to all these and more have been carefully provided in this book. Read on. Enjoy yourself.

THE PURPOSE OF THIS BOOK

The purpose of this book is to help the reader discover and acknowledge the hidden mysteries of the Virgin Mary and her indispensable position in the economy of salvation. For there are so many other things that were done by Jesus Christ which are not written down in the Bible Jn. 20:30; 3 Jn.13-14. Therefore let no one judge in a human way what is done in a divine mystery. Let no one try to penetrate this heavenly mystery by earthly reasoning. Let no one treat this novel secret from knowledge of everyday occurrences. Let no one manipulate the work of love into an insult, or run the risk of losing faith.

C H A P T E R   1

MARY
MOTHER AND QUEEN
CHOSEN BEFORE CREATION

Before creating the human race, God had created a woman in his divine mind and chosen her to become the conquest of Satan and rescue to man. He told the angels that he was going to create a human nature in his own image and likeness, and from these creatures he would create a queen, to stand on the right of his throne and govern with him all creatures *Gen. 1: 26 27; Ps 45: 9 14*. He told them that he was going to elevate humanity to the height of *'Divine Personality'* by way of the *'Incarnation'* of the Second Person of the Blessed Trinity. That is to say, God the Son would assume human nature from the promised queen so that God and man would become one. This union by which God and man would become one, this union by which Divinity and Humanity would become one, is what we call the *'Hypostatic union'*. It took place in the immaculate womb of the promised queen. On account of this, God decreed that man should not only acknowledge him as their Head and God, but also as God and Man, and adore Him as God-Man.

He also decreed that the promised queen shall become the channel through which divine graces would be distributed to the human race. Therefore, she should be called the 'Mediatrix' of all graces. Again, He decreed that all creatures, both angels and men, must honour, serve, and proclaim her blessed - *Ps. 45: 17; Prov. 31: 31; Lk. 1: 48; Judith 13: 18 20*. But while the angels were rejoicing and thanking God for this, Lucifer, who was then next to God, became proud and envious. He felt an injury had been done to his greatness because God had made him inferior to the Queen, and so refused to honour her and induced his followers to disobey likewise. This is the true story of the disobedience of Lucifer in heaven. This is the reason why some people honour Mary today and some others do not. Lucifer was so furious and frustrated that he boasted to attack the woman and her children, and to make them enemies of God.

On account of this, God became angry and said to him: *"This woman whom you have refused to honour shall crush your head to pieces"*, and if through your pride death enters into the world, I tell you, through her humility, life and salvation shall enter into the world so that those who shall honour and serve her as their mother and queen, shall enjoy the gifts and crowns which you and your followers have lost. In the end, Lucifer was thrown out of heaven as a fallen angel, and from that moment he became a tempter, or Satan, or serpent, or dragon. In the book of Revelation, chapter twelve *(Rev. 12)*, we shall see this great battle going on.

In creating the human race, God concealed from Lucifer how and when God the Son was to assume human nature, and how and when Adam and Eve were to be created, so that he might labour ignorantly from the beginning regarding the mystery and the time of the Incarnation. And because God had said the promised queen shall become the mother of God the Son, Lucifer thought that a woman was to be created first, and man, second. But God in his own wisdom, created man, Adam, first, and from man he created the woman, Eve *Gen. 2: 7-23.* When Satan saw these people, he suspected Adam to be Jesus Christ, and Eve to be the Virgin Mary, the promised Queen. He suspected Eve to be the mother of Adam and so concluded that Adam was God the Son. Therefore, he could not deceive him. This was the reason why he did not go to Adam. Rather, he moved straight away to Eve, tempted her, and deceived her into eating the forbidden fruit *Gen. 3: 6.*

After the woman had eaten the fruit, she took some and gave to Adam, and together, they disobeyed God. The glory and grace of God in man was lost. From that moment, their offspring multiplied into the good and the bad, or the elect and the reprobates, or the followers of God and Mary, and the followers of Satan. Followers of Satan persecuted followers of God and Mary as was the case of Cain and Abel, and Esau and Jacob *Gen. 4:2-10; Gen. 27:41.* This persecution has continued till date and we all experience it everyday, *Rev. 12:17,*but our hope is that, in the end, the Immaculate Heart of Mary must triumph. We shall all celebrate the victory.

While Satan continued to celebrate his victory over the woman, Eve, not long, God repeated to him that same threat he had already heard in heaven, *"The woman shall crush your head to pieces"?*

Children of God, we are now entering into Mary in the Bible, proper.

C H A P T E R 2

MARY
THE WOMAN OF PROMISE, PROPHECY AND LIBERATION

Genesis 3: 15.

In this portion of the Bible, God says to Satan, *"I will put enmity between you and the woman, and between your seed and her seed, she will crush your head and you will bite her heel"*. By this eternal decree, God promises to send a second woman who shall come as a conquest of Satan and rescue to men. He wills that since his glory and grace in man was lost through the first woman, Eve, who was deceived and conquered by Satan, the second woman shall be supernaturally powerful as to crush the head of Satan to pieces so that his glory and grace would be restored in man.

When Satan heard this threat, he began to laugh at God because he knew he had already conquered a woman but he did not know that the woman God was actually talking about, was still on the way and not Eve.

At this juncture, I want everyone to take note of the word 'Woman'. As Satan continued to labour in ignorance and confusion, the prophets began to prophesy on the restoration of the glory of God to man and the salvation of the human race.

Micah 5: 2 5. In this portion of the Bible, a woman was promised and awaited to bear a son so that the Lord who had abandoned the humankind due to the disobedience (sin) of the first woman, Eve, would now come back to them and bring peace. The Bible reads: "So the Lord will abandon his people to their enemies (Satan and his agents) until the woman who is pregnant has her son. Then his fellow countrymen who are in exile will be reunited with their own people. When he comes, he will rule his people with the Majesty of God himself. His people will live in safety; they will acknowledge his greatness and he will bring peace".

By this statement, the promised and awaited woman now serves as a means of reconciliation or peace making between God and man between heaven and earth - between divinity and humanity. She thus reconciles all mankind with their creator. Therefore, anyone who truly wants to be reconciled with God, must go straight away to her yet, we do not know her name because the Bible calls her woman.

Isaiah 7: 14. In this portion of the Bible, the prophet Isaiah explaining to Ahaz the king of Judah (and in a sense, to all the human family), about the sign of Immanuel the sign of salvation, has this to say: Therefore, the Lord himself will give us a sign, *"Behold, a woman, indeed, a virgin, shall conceive, and bear a son and shall call his name Immanuel".* While Immanuel means God is with us *Mtt. 1: 23,* Isaiah means Yahweh is salvation. This prophecy of Isaiah shows that this woman would become a sign of liberation to mankind a sign of hope for the hungry and the down trodden a sign of light to the world a light full of holiness and love a light that clears away darkness a light full of glory and grace the sun - shine of heaven and earth a great sign of salvation and victory of God over every form of evil and sin.

Jeremiah 31:22. Here, the Bible says that God will create a new thing upon the earth: *"A woman shall compass (or protect) a man".* If we should explain this prophecy a little, we will discover that when the Blessed Virgin Mary conceived Jesus Christ in her womb, she carried and protected him in the form of God man. And when Satan in the person of Herod wanted to kill the infant Jesus, Mary protected his life in Egypt. In this way, Jeremiah's prophecy is fulfilled *Mt. 2: 13 15.*

This protective task signaled how all God's own people the faithful followers of the gospel, will in imitation of their master Jesus according to *Mt. 11: 29,* fly to the patronage of this great woman of promise and she will become their refuge, to protect and defend them against the attack and subtle snares of the enemy or the red dragon, and to fight for them against his dominion. This way, she accomplishes her task of being the means of achieving God's victory over every form of evil and sin.

Song of Songs 6: 8 10. Here, a revelation of a woman was made to King Solomon, and because she appeared with incomparable or perfect beauty and was as lovely as a dove, moving in power and glory, all women including queens and concubines looked at her and praised her. King Solomon was moved to ask, *"Who is this woman that cometh forth as the Morning Rising, fair as the Moon, bright as the Sun, terrible as an Army set in battle array?"* The reason why she appeared as an army ready for a battle was to confirm that she will battle to crush Satan to pieces. Yet we do not know her name because the Bible only calls her woman.

Revelation 12: 1. A revelation of the same woman shown to Solomon in the Old Testament is again shown to St. John in the New Testament. John looked up to the sky and saw an incomparably beautiful woman whose dress was the sun, a crown of twelve stars on her head, and the moon under her feet. The sun, the stars, and the moon imply that she is completely covered with light. That is to say, she was conceived and born immaculate and there is no stain of sin in her, neither original nor actual because she is full of grace *Lk. 1: 28; Lk. 1: 30.* The twelve stars on her head represent the twelve tribes of Israel, the twelve apostles upon whom the Catholic Church was founded by Jesus of Nazareth, the Catholic Priests and all those who accept the woman as their mother and queen. The crown on her head shows that she is a queen that great queen whom God had spoken about in heaven.

Galatians 4: 4 5. In this portion of the Bible, St. Paul says, *"When the right time for salvation finally came, Jesus Christ the Son of God came as the Son of a human mother and lived under the law so that we all might become sons and daughters of God".*

St. Paul emphasizes on the need for this spiritual adoption by Jesus' Mother because before then, man was a slave of sin due to the disobedience of the first woman, Eve. But with this spiritual adoption, man is now set free since it is by a woman free of sin: a woman who was destined from eternity to give birth to a son who will set all men free from sin. It was not until at the fullness of time that this woman who was not known to anybody became known through the message of the Angel Gabriel - *Lk. 1: 26 31.* Although God being Almighty could still have devised another means to save mankind other than by sending his beloved son taken from a woman, to come and suffer for us. He did not do so because it had been his will to make use of that worthy but very humble mother. Therefore, if we believe Jesus to be our brother, his mother must become our mother, and his father also becomes our father. Hence we are no longer slaves but sons and daughters of God. Anyone who is not adopted by this great woman of promise will have no claim on the side of God because Jesus Christ must be the first among many brothers and sisters, and his mother, the mother of all *Rm. 8:*

29; Heb. 2: 11 12; Gal. 4: 30 31.

Isaiah 66: 7 10. In this biblical quotation, God promises to send a second woman into the world, through whom all his people would come back to him as a nation and he would become their God once again. Therefore, *"A woman shall become the Most Holy City of God, by conceiving and bearing a son, and so shall become the mother of all"*. The Bible then concludes that, those who shall obey the son and remain faithful to him shall in turn become sons and daughters of the mother. They shall form a nation to be ruled by the son. If we go to the book of *Rev. 12: 5,* we shall see the son ruling that nation. So also is the book of *Rev. 19: 13 16.* Then God asks: *"Has anyone ever seen or heard or comprehended such a thing: that a nation is born in a day by a woman?"* - *Isaiah 66: 8.*

Children of God, a nation is said to be born in a day by a woman because, by giving birth to a son (Jesus Christ) through whom a new nation of God's own people would emerge, she has therefore, given birth to a nation the new Israel the Catholic Church a chosen race the king's priests a holy nation God's own people a people set apart to sing the praises of God who called them out of darkness into his wonderful light *1Pt. 2: 9 10; Heb. 8: 8 13.* For this reason, the Bible refers to her as 'Mother Zion': an ideal for the future: the hope of the people of God: the past, the present and the future.

In conclusion, God says that we should embrace this

wonderful privilege with great joy and thankfulness. He also says that all those who love this Holy City, this great woman of promise, should rejoice with her and be glad for her *Is. 66:10.*

Proverbs 8: 35 36. Here, the scripture says: *"The man who finds the promised woman (who is hereby symbolized by wisdom) finds life, and the Lord will be pleased with him. The man who does not find her hurts himself; anyone who hates her loves death".*

Great Saints and Doctors of the Church such as St. Louis Marie De Montfort agree with this biblical explanation. The reason why the Bible is insisting that the only way we can find life is by finding this great woman of promise, prophecy and liberation, is because since Jesus Christ the fruit of her womb is life, she herself has automatically and fittingly become the tree of life *Prov. 3: 18.* Therefore, for anyone to find real life, he or she must begin by finding the source of life which is that great woman of promise. She is the tree whose fruit brings life.

Wisdom 6: 13. Here, the Bible concludes that this woman so far promised and prophesied about as a conquest of Satan and rescue to men, can only be found by those who truly love her and search for her. It reads: *"She is easily seen by those that love her, and is found by them that seek her".* That is to say, he who does not seek her can never find her, and he who does not know her can never seek her, for no one can seek or desire what he does not know. But since finding the woman means finding life, we all should learn to know her, to love her, and to seek her, so that we can find the end we are seeking which is Jesus Christ our life *Jn. 1:4; Jn. 14: 6; Jn. 11: 25.* She is the source of life because Jesus did not fall down straight away from heaven. Rather, he passed through her to come to us and decrees that we should also pass through her to come to him *Jn. 19: 26 27.* She is the sure means, the straight and the immaculate way to go to Jesus yet we do not know her name because the Bible only calls her *'Woman'.*

Now let us visit the house of Joachim and Anne, the parents of the Blessed Virgin Mary.

C H A P T E R 3

MARY
THE ROLES OF JOACHIM AND ANNE,
THE PARENTS OF MARY

In the Old Israel, there was a man named Joachim, from Nazareth, a town in Galilee. He was holy and prayerful. He had knowledge of the Holy Scriptures and had always prayed God for the coming of the promised Messiah. There was also a woman named Anne, from Bethlehem. She, too, was holy and prayerful. She also had knowledge of the Holy Scriptures and had always prayed God for the coming of the promised Messiah. At the time Joachim was praying for a good and God fearing wife, Anne was in Bethlehem, praying for a good and God fearing husband. Joachim never thought of Anne becoming his wife, and Anne never thought of Joachim becoming her husband. By divine selection, they became husband and wife. Anne was about twenty four at the time and Joachim was forty two. While Joachim means "Yahweh saves", Anne means "Grace".

Every year these couple would go to the temple in Jerusalem

to make sacrifices to God, praying for the coming of the promised Messiah. They also prayed God to give them a child and promised to consecrate it to the service of God in the temple, after three years.

There was this particular year, when the number of the people making sacrifice became too much for the priests in the temple. So, the priests resorted to making selection. But when Joachim and Anne took their sacrifices to the priests, they rejected them. They humiliated them before the people, and even asked them to leave the temple, saying that God has rejected them. But God did not reject them. In tears and sorrows, they moved separately to different ends of the temple and prayed, accepting their humiliation as a result of their unworthiness. Joachim prayed God to have mercy on them; to give them a child and take away their disgrace. Anne also prayed God: *"O my God, our disgrace has been doubled. You have not given us a child; again, your priests have rejected our sacrifice. Please, let people not call us barren"*. In the end, they left the temple as people laughed and mocked at them. When they got home, not long, the Angel Gabriel appeared to Anne and said: *"Anne, Anne, wipe your tears and cry no more, for God has answered your prayers. You will conceive and bear a baby girl, and you will call her name Mary. She will grow to become the mother of the long awaited Messiah but do not tell this to your husband"*. In the night, the Angel appeared to Joachim in a dream and assured him of a child. In the morning, Joachim called Anne and told her about the dream and she replied that she, too, had the same dream.

Joachim became sterile after their first child, Mary Heli, whom as they found out was not the child of promise. For about twenty years after Mary Heli's birth, they remained childless. They lived in continued prayer, sacrifice, mortification, and continence, and away from each other. They kept to this through all the years. And those were their most painful years of marriage. People had within those years insulted them; humiliated them, dejected them, and gossiped about them. For all those that were childless were considered by the people as excluded from the benefits of the Messiah. In the then Jewish world, childlessness was seen as a curse, a reproach, an affliction, and a great sorrow. Barren women were humiliated, dejected, mocked at, and even relegated to the background by their fellow women *Gen. 30: 1; 1Sam 6: 1 11; Isaiah 4: 1; Lk. 1: 24 25*. This was exactly what the holy couple, Joachim and Anne, suffered through. People even treated them as divorcees not knowing that their reason for not staying together as husband and wife during this period, was to keep to their promise of *continence*, that is, a period of abstinence from sexual intercourse because a goat does not stay with a yam. No matter how little that goat may be, it will eat up the yam.

At this juncture, let us take into consideration the transmission of God's mysterious blessing, the blessing of the Immaculate Conception from the first man, Adam, down to St. Joachim, the father of the Virgin Mary (according to the Life of Jesus Christ and Biblical Revelations to Blessed

Catherine Emmerich, 1774-1824).

After the creation of Adam, God created Eve, by taking a rib from the right side of Adam, from the same place in which the side of Jesus was opened by the lance. In place of the rib, God filled the space with a luminous body, a mysterious blessing. Adam alone was given this special blessing. It was the Germ of God's blessing. It was meant for a pure and holy multiplication of the human race, that is, a type of multiplication that was to arise out of God, from God, and by God. Adam and Eve were created immaculate, that is, without sin. Also, they were to reproduce immaculately, without sin. They had already received the command from God to increase and multiply, but they did not know as yet how this was going to be accomplished. In order to counter the plan of God, Satan deceived Eve into eating the forbidden fruit. This, the woman gave the husband, and the glory of God in man was lost. This is the fall of man.

Enclosed in Adam and Eve, was the corporal and spiritual life of all men. By the fall the life became corrupted, mixed up with evil, and was overpowered by the bad angels. But before Adam had sinned, the Second Person of the Most Blessed Trinity, came down from heaven, and took away from him the Germ of God's blessing. This way, the blessing was withdrawn from Adam. It was preserved from being stained. It was later bestowed upon Noah, and from Noah it got to Abraham during the visit of the angels. But it was given to him in a veiled manner, and was more like a pledge of fulfillment of the promise that he should be the father of all nations-*Gen. 17:1-6; Gen. 18:1-15.*

Abraham was to bestow the blessing upon Isaac. On the other hand, Isaac was to bestow the blessing upon Jacob-*Gen. 27:27-29.*

It was to be withdrawn from Jacob after he had become a nation. Then, the blessing would be restored again and placed in the Ark of the Covenant as a *'holy thing'* belonging to the whole nation. The blessing was withdrawn from Jacob at the time he wrestled with an angel of God who eventually changed his name to Israel-*Gen.32:22-29.* At last it was bestowed upon Joseph (the name Joseph is a shortened expression of the traditional Hebrew name *Johoseph,* which basically means *"may Yahweh give an increase"*).

In the person of Potiphar's wife, Satan continued in his struggle to destroy the Germ of God's blessing which he could not do before Adam had sinned. But Joseph maintained his chastity; refusing to commit the sin of the flesh. He died with the blessing and was buried with it-*Gen. 39:6-10.*

On the eve of their departure from Egypt, the mystery was removed from Joseph's remains by the Israelites and Moses took possession of it. Since then it has always been kept in the Ark of the Covenant because it now belongs to the entire Jewish nation. Eventually, the mysterious blessing was bestowed upon Joachim, that the Blessed Virgin, the living Ark of the Covenant, might be conceived as pure and stainless, as Eve was upon coming forth from the side of Adam. This is the transmission of Adam's blessing, the blessing of a pure and holy multiplication of the human race, through out the ages, through the ancestry of Jesus Christ down to Joachim and Anne, the parents of Mary.

There was this particular year when the Israelites were to assemble in the temple in Jerusalem. This time, the Holy Spirit moved the priests in the temple to accept Joachim's offerings. Two priests conducted him into the Holy Place, and left him there alone, after burning incense on the altar. As he was praying, all of a sudden, the Angel Gabriel appeared and told him not to grieve any more over his sterility. For this was not a disgrace to him but a great honour and glory. For the child who was to be born of his wife would be the most perfect flower of the race of Abraham. That the conception of the child should not be from him but through him; a fruit from God, the culminating point of Abraham's blessing. God had already removed from Joachim all sensualities.

Now the Angel removed something from the Ark of the Covenant without opening the door (because since the Ark is a symbol of Mary, the door is a symbol of Mary's perpetual virginity). It was the mystery of the Ark, the Sacrament of the Incarnation, the Immaculate Conception, the consummation of Abraham's blessing. It was a luminous body. He anointed Joachim's fore head, and slipped the shining body under his garment and it entered into his body. The Angel also gave him something to drink out of a glittering chalice. From that moment, the mystery got missing from the Ark of the Covenant. In the end, Joachim was left alone at the Golden Gate of the Temple, where his wife (Anne) was to meet him.

St. Anne had just made her offering in another part of the temple. As she could not find Joachim, she became worried. Not long, the Angel Gabriel appeared to her and said: *"Anne, the favoured one of God; hurry up to the golden gate. There, you will find Joachim"*. When she got to the gate, behold, Joachim was there. At once, they embraced themselves in tears of happiness and love. For they had not seen each other for a long time. The heaven opened, the Most Blessed Trinity smiled on them and covered them with a dazzling light. And they were rapted in ecstasy. It was within this holy embrace that God miraculously cleansed, sanctified, blessed and consecrated the womb of Anne, making it holy and worthy for the immediate conception of the Most Blessed Virgin Mary. God also used this holy embrace to clear away from the minds of the people, the false belief that Joachim and Anne had been divorced. He did this in order to safeguard the pregnancy so that people would not stone Anne to death, thinking that she might have committed adultery since she had not been with Joachim for a long time. Also, by the holy embrace God wanted to protect the image of the Virgin Mary; that she would not appear to the people as a bastard.

She was conceived immaculately, that is, without sin.

By this account we could see that the individuals through whom the transmission of God's mysterious blessing was done were only made to hold the blessing in proxy, pending the time when the rightful owner, the Virgin Mary, would have been created. At the appointed time this whole blessing was used to mould her in the womb of Anne. In other words, she is the blessings of God, the fullness of God's divine grace put in human form.

The lesson of the Immaculate Conception shows that, though sexual conception is allowed by God, only to be used by sacramentally married couples; it is not to be done in a sinful way.

No wonder Jesus said to Maria Valtorta in the Poem of the Man-God: *"My daughter, God had created man and woman with such a perfect law of love that you cannot even understand its perfection any longer. And you become lost in wondering how the human species would have come to be if Adam and Eve did not fornicate. Who told you I wanted man to reproduce in a sinful and painful way? Had you been faithful to God, you would have had the joy of children, in a holy way, without pain, without exhausting yourselves in obscene and shameful intercourses".*

From all eternity God had created Mary's soul immaculate. It was always in the light and knowledge of God. It was never deprived of the closeness and remembrance of God, of his wisdom, his grace and love. The Blessed Virgin was therefore, able to love and understand, even when she was just a flesh forming around an immaculate soul. She was conceived in the original holiness and justice. That is to say, she had a supernatural inward gift or a superadded fullness of grace given to her from the very first moment of her personal existence. If we truly believe that Eve was raised above human nature by that indwelling moral gift which we call grace from the very moment of her being and she destroyed it by disobedience, is it not fitting that God would have bestowed upon the Blessed Virgin this same supernatural privilege from the very moment of her being since her office and position would be that of the second Eve? Again, we all know that John the Baptist had an immaculate birth, for he was given the grace of God three months before his birth, at the time the Holy Virgin visited his mother *Lk. 1: 36* and *41*. He was not accordingly, immaculately conceived because he was alive before grace came to him, but Mary's case only differs from his in this respect: that grace came to her not when she was already existing nor three months before her birth, but from the very first moment of her being, as it had been given to Eve. Oh, if only we understood what grace means. The Protestants (i.e. non-Catholics) believe grace to be a mere external approbation or acceptance, whereas it is a real inward condition, a superadded quality of soul. And the Blessed Virgin had a greater grace. She was conceived without any transmission of original sin; for there is nothing God cannot do - *Mk.10: 27; Lk. 1: 37.* This is what we call the *Immaculate Conception.* This consideration gives significance to the Angel's salutation of Mary as *Full of Grace Lk. 1:28.*

At this juncture, non-Catholics may be tempted to ask the question: How does this consideration enable us to say that Mary was conceived without original sin since she, too, is a descendant of the fallen Adam?

Children of God, this privilege or doctrine has no reference whatever to her parents, but simply to her own person as the second Eve. If non-Catholics knew what we mean by original sin, they would not ask the question. The Catholic doctrine of original sin is not the same as the protestant doctrine. With the Catholic Church, *"Original Sin"* cannot be called sin in the ordinary sense of the word *"Sin".* It is a term denoting the imputation of the sin of Adam. That is to say, the state to which the sin of Adam reduces humanity. But by Protestants, it is understood to be sin in the same sense as actual sin. While the Catholics think of it as something negative, the Protestants think of it as something positive. They hold that it is a disease a change of nature a poison internally corrupting the soul and propagated from father to son after the manner of a bad constitution. They accuse us (Catholics) of ascribing a different nature from ours to the Most Blessed Virgin: different from that of her parents, and from that of the fallen Adam. But this is not true because we consider that in Adam she died as others; that she was included together with the whole human race in the sentence of Adam: that she incurred his debt as we do; but that for the sake of Him who was to redeem man upon the cross, her own debt was remitted by *anticipation;* the general sentence on mankind was not carried out on her, except indeed as regards her natural death, for she died as others when it was her time.

Mary was free from original sin. She was completely exempted from it by the eternal decree of God. She was given this special privilege in order to fit her to become the mother of the Redeemer. From all eternity God decreed to create the human race and fore-seeing the fall of Adam, He decreed to redeem the whole race by the son's taking flesh and suffering on the cross. In that same incomprehensible eternal instant, in which the Son of God was born of the Father, was also the decree which was passed of man's redemption through him. He, who was born from eternity, was born by an eternal decree to save us in time and to redeem the whole race; and Mary's redemption was determined in that special manner which we call the Immaculate Conception. It was decreed not that she should be cleansed from sin, but that, from the very moment of her being she should be preserved from sin; so that Satan never had any part in her. Therefore, she was a child of Adam and Eve as if they had never fallen. This is what we call the *Immaculate Conception* of the Most Blessed Virgin Mary. And we celebrate the feast every December 8th *the feast of the Solemnity of the Immaculate Conception.*

The doctrine of the Immaculate Conception is a dogma of the Catholic Church. That is to say, an official doctrine of the Church, an article of faith. This doctrine was formally and dogmatically defined, on December 8, 1854, by His Holiness, Pope Pius IX.

Mary was conceived and born without sin, that she might better co- operate in the saving work of Christ. She remains perpetually sinless due to the following reasons:

That the serpent or dragon shall at no time boast of being superior to the woman whom God will obey as his true mother.

That the human flesh, from which the Word is to assume form, must be free from sin. Since He is to redeem in it sinners, he must not be under the necessity of redeeming his own flesh, like that of sinners.

That Jesus Christ has at no time being in enmity with his own flesh.
Sons and daughters of God and Mary, the Blessed Virgin was not only conceived immaculately, she is the immaculate Conception itself. For she was moulded and formed by God in the womb of Anne by that mysterious blessing of the Ark, that luminous body, that blessing given to Adam and withdrawn from him, the Immaculate Conception. Thus she told Saint Bernadette at Lourdes: "I am the Immaculate Conception".

Now, having carried her baby for 9 months within her womb, St. Anne later gave birth to Mary, the *masterpiece* of God's creation, the true *reflection* of his divine perfection. After 3years, they offered her to the service of God in the temple. In the temple, Mary conquered all temptations of the enemy because she is full of grace. By divine selection, she married Joseph. And by the power of the Holy Spirit, she conceived Jesus Christ in her womb and bore him into the world as *God-man*, and the promise of God in heaven was fulfilled.

On one occasion, during the preaching of Jesus Christ some Pharisees asked him about the missing blessing of the Ark which had now been used to form the Blessed Virgin Mary and the Blessed fruit of her womb, Jesus. So, he said to them, *"The fact that the blessing is missing shows that the Messiah has already come"*. By this, Jesus meant that He is the Blessing of the Ark; the blessing that they were looking for, but they could not understand Him.

Children of God, remember we are still searching to know who actually is that person whom the Bible refers to as woman beginning from Genesis to Revelation. Now let us visit the letter of Saint John, chapter two, verses three and four *(Jn. 2: 3 4)*. In this portion of the Bible, Jesus shows us the woman, the promised Queen, the Conquest of Satan and Rescue to man.

Jesus Shows Us The Woman

In the gospel according to *Jn. 2: 3 - 4*, Jesus and Mary were at a wedding feast of Cana in Galilee. All of a sudden the wine got finished. At once Mary moved straight away to Jesus and said, *"Son, they have no wine left"*. Then Jesus got up and said to her, *"Woman, what do you want from me? Do you not know that my hour has not yet come?"* Jesus did not call her mother and neither did he call her Mary, rather he called her woman. The reason why he addressed her by the word *"woman"* was to maintain the same word by which the Bible describes her beginning from Genesis to Revelation. He acted accordingly so as to identify Mary as the Woman of promise and the woman of prophecy who, together with him, would bring God's glory to man. He knew that people at the occasion came from different parts of the world. So, by publicly and deliberately addressing his Blessed Mother as woman, he specifically wanted everyone (including you and me), to recognize and acknowledge her as that woman promised by God, to conquer Satan and rescue the human family. She is that great Queen whom God had spoken about in heaven.

CHAPTER 4

MARY
MOTHER OF CHRIST AND OURS

Many Christians do not know the extent to which the Blessed Virgin is their mother. You call her mother and so you think you know. But you have only very little idea of her motherhood in your regard. You love her as if she were your mother. If I may ask, what will your mother answer you, if you say to her: I love you as if you were my mother? Your guess is as good as mine. Oh, this is how you love and honour your heavenly mother.

You think that Mary is your mother solely in virtue of the words spoken by Jesus on the cross with regard to her before he died: *"Woman, behold your son, son, behold your mother"*. Although these words confided a maternal mission to Mary, her motherhood in your regard never depended on them. Otherwise, it would have become a mere adoptive motherhood.

Mary is your true mother in the supernatural and spiritual order just as your earthly mothers are your true mothers in the natural and corporal order. A mother is one who gives life to its child and Mary has given you the most real life Jesus Christ himself *Jn. 1: 4; Jn. 14: 6; Jn 11: 25*. There are three major ways by which the Virgin Mary has given you life and so become your true mother, namely:

At Nazareth: Mary gave you life, for in conceiving Jesus who is life she also conceived you. When the Angel Gabriel brought a message of salvation to her, she knew that by answering 'Yes' or 'No', she would either give you life or leave you in death. Yes, because she is indispensable in God's plan of salvation. No one else could have been chosen had she rejected the task. In *Heb 10: 5*, Jesus says: *"I thank you Father, because you have prepared a body for me"*. That body was the body of the Most Blessed Virgin Mary in whom the word was made flesh and dwelt among us. By the word *"Prepared"*, it implies that she had been destined from eternity to become the Mother of Jesus and our means of Salvation. Thus if she had rejected the task, salvation would not have come to man, that is to say, you would have remained in death. But because she had some ideas of the design of God to man and also wanted you (and me) to live she answered Yes, *"Behold, the handmaid of the Lord. Be it done unto me according to your word"* - *Lk 1: 38*. A reply so sweet to the hearing of God and so fortunate for mankind. At that moment, the Holy Spirit overshadowed her and Jesus was conceived in her womb. By consenting to give human life to Jesus, at the same time, she consented to give spiritual life to you. In other words, in becoming Christ's mother, she became your (our) mother. From that moment, you constituted parts of Christ's Mystical Body which is the Church. Jesus was the head and you were the members *Rm. 8: 29; Jn. 15: 5; 1Cor. 12: 27 28; Eph. 5: 30*. And since no woman can be a mother to a head without a body or a body without a head (for such a child would become a monster), the Virgin Mary must become the mother of all. That is to say, she must become the mother of both Jesus (the head) and you (the members) *Isaiah 66: 7 10; Gal. 4: 30 31; Rev. 12: 17*. She bore you and Jesus in her maternal womb, but in different ways. She bore Jesus according to the flesh and you according to the spirit. So, while she has become Christ's physical mother, she has become your spiritual mother.

In the book of Song of Songs, the Bible says: *"What a wonderful girl you are O Prince daughter, your belly is like a heap of wheat encircled with lilies" - Songs 7: 1 2*. The Blessed Virgin Mary is the Prince daughter *Ps 45: 10 14*. And although in her most pure womb, there was but one grain of corn which was Jesus Christ, yet it is called a heap of wheat because the rest of God's own children you and me the brothers and sisters of Jesus Christ, were also contained in it as Mary was to be their mother also.

At Baptism: The second way by which the Virgin Mary has become your true mother is by way of baptism. Baptism is the first step to salvation *Jn. 3: 5; Mk. 16: 16.* It is a sacrament which cleanses us from original sin, makes us Christians, children of God, and members of the Church.

As long as the supernatural world was concerned, your natural mothers brought you into the world as *"yet to be born".* For you to come to real life, sanctifying grace had to be infused into you at baptism. This sanctifying grace came to you by means of Mary *Full of Grace.* For without Mary no grace is ever given. When you were born into the world, you became children of death due to the sin of Adam and Eve. You needed transformation into children of life. That transformation was done at baptism and so you became brothers and sisters of Jesus Christ *Rm 6: 3 4.* It was the Virgin Mary who bore you into that life of grace of God and so became your true mother in the supernatural order.

Baptism is meant for everyone, both adults and infants. It is unfortunate that some Christians have continued to reject and fight against infant baptism, this truth which is rooted in the Bible and clarified by the Church's tradition. They argue that little children should not be baptized until they have become adults, on the grounds that they should first of all understand what baptism is all about. For Jesus Christ himself was baptized when he was already an adult. If I may ask, should we say that Jesus was baptized because he was a sinner like us? Of course not. He was baptized not to be cleansed from sin, but to teach us what we must do. For in this way, we shall do all that God requires. He is the one who takes away the sin of the world *Mt. 3: 13-15; Jn. 1: 29.*

My Questions: Are little children not infected by original sin the sin of Adam and Eve? Have you not read in the Bible that all men (both adults and infants) have sinned and fallen short of God's grace *Rm 3: 23?* Does death not kill little children until they have become adults? Are little children not included in the benefits of baptism, tell me? Is it not in your Bible that Jesus himself requests his disciples to bring little children to him? *Mt. 19: 13 15; Mk 10: 13 16; Lk 18: 15 17.*

Now let me refer you to some passages in the Bible where adult and infant baptism took place. In *Acts 10: 47- 48*, a captain in the Roman Army named Cornelius was baptized by Peter along with his entire household. In *Acts 16: 31-34*, St. Paul baptizes a man named Crispus who was a leader of the synagogue, together with his entire household. In *Acts 16: 15*, St. Paul again baptizes a woman called Lydia together with her entire household. This type of baptism is what we call *"Household Baptism"*. What is household? A household is a composition of persons living in one same family. It comprises of father, mother and children. It includes also relatives and house helps, as long as they live in the same house. Household Baptism is therefore, the baptism of both parents and children, that is, the baptism of both adults and infants. There is no age limit. So, anyone who goes about preaching against infant baptism is going contrary to the gospel of Jesus Christ. He is a man of bad doctrine a heretic a reprobate an anti-Christ.

On Calvary: The third and final way by which the Blessed Virgin Mary has become the Mother of all Christians, is by way of the event on Calvary. On Calvary, she gave life to you by offering Jesus on the cross. She conceived him as a victim and offered him as a sacrifice in order that you might live. By Christ's death on the cross, you were delivered from sin and death and so merited the grace of living the life of God.

At his death, Jesus has wanted Mary's presence in order that he might make with her but one same sacrifice and be immolated to the eternal father by her consent just as Isaac of old was offered by Abraham's consent to the will of God. By offering Jesus to God, Mary renounced her maternal rights over him. She, who experienced joy in the birth of Jesus, experienced the most agonizing sorrows in your birth. This is the consummation of Mary's motherhood in your regard. At this juncture, Jesus confided John to Mary, and Mary to John: *"Woman, behold your son, son, behold your Mother" Jn 19: 26 27.* But these words did not create that motherhood rather they proclaimed, attested, confirmed and completed it. This was Christ's last '*Will*' and '*Testament*' on earth the gift of his beloved Mother to the human race.

In *verse 27*, the Bible says that Jesus gave his Blessed Mother to the disciple. If I may ask, who is a disciple of Jesus Christ? A disciple of Christ is a true follower of Christ, a Christian *Acts 11: 26.* The reason why the word '*disciple*' is used instead of John, who was at the foot of the cross with Mary, is because it is not applicable to John alone but to all Christians. John was there to represent you and me the entire Christendom. This implies that Mary is given to all Christians, to be taken care of, and she, to take care of them. Again, the Bible says from that moment, the disciple took Mary to live in his home. The word *"home"* as used in the context, does not refer to our earthly home, rather it symbolizes the *"heart"* of a true disciple. Oh, how great must be the joy of Christ when we as his disciples, give Mary a special place to dwell in our hearts the true home of Jesus and Mary. Jesus has willed that in the same way as Mary led him on the way to Calvary and prayerfully stood by him at the foot of the cross, she may also lead us in carrying our individual crosses both corporal and spiritual, while offering prayers to God on our behalf. And as she does this, she proves that she is the *"Help of Christians"*.

Finally, Mary's presence at Christ's death confirms that God, who started his greatest works by Mary, has now ended it also by Mary. This goes to show that all Christians the true Imitators of Christ according to *Mt. 11: 29*, shall also need Mary's presence at the hour of their death. No wonder the church has continued to encourage her faithful children to always pray to Mary: *"Holy Mary, Mother of God, pray for us sinners now, and at the hour of our death, amen"*. Oh, how many times have we repeated this prayer to Mary as we recite the Holy Rosary! This is an invocation that draws her very close to us, especially at the hour of our death that great hour when we need the grace of God most. With great joy she listens to it and answers it. With the splendour of her glorified body she receives our souls into her motherly arms and brings them to Jesus her son for his particular judgment. Children of God, think how joyful must be the meeting of Jesus Christ with those souls who are presented to him by his very own mother. The joy will be great because Mary herself will cover them with her own holiness, give them the innocence of her purity and the white robe of her charity, and where there remains some stain, she quickly wipes it away and gives them that brightness that holiness that immaculateness which will enable them to become real citizens of heaven.

My dear people of God, you are the brothers and sisters of Jesus Christ because his father is your father, and his mother is your mother. Just as in the natural and corporal generation of children, there are a father and a mother, so in the supernatural and spiritual generation, there a father who is God, and a mother who is Mary. All true Christians, all members of God's household which is the church, must have God for their father, and Mary for their mother. For God Himself must have a complete household. Heaven is therefore, a complete spiritual home *Eph. 3: 15*. Only in hell do we have motherless children or incomplete spiritual home because the Virgin Mary is not there. Hell is therefore, a spiritual motherless home.

Brethren, the Virgin Mary is even more truly your mother than your earthly mothers due to the manner in which she has given you life and the nature of the life she gave to you. For while your earthly mothers gave you life full of imperfections, sorrows and limitations a created life, Mary gave you life full of perfections, happiness and endlessness life uncreated Jesus Christ Himself life of sharing in the eternity and in the beatitude of God the life of the Most Blessed Trinity. While your earthly mothers stop looking after you the moment you become adults, Mary continues to look after you until Christ is formed in you. While your earthly mothers grieve and weep helplessly over your corpses, Mary can restore life to you if you are to loose your eternal life unhappily. She loves you more than your earthly mothers because her love surpasses all others in intensity and in purity. Now you can see that Mary did not just give you life, rather she brought you forth to life. What human motherhood could compare with such motherhood?

All children of God must admire and appreciate Mary's motherhood in their regard. They must accept Mary as their own true mother, and must abandon themselves completely to her in the same way as Jesus did. That is, with the simplicity of children listening to their mother, they will not ask why she (Mary) speaks, or how she speaks, or where her words are going to lead them. They love her and listen to her. They let themselves be formed and led by her words, as they grow each day in life. This way, their hearts inflame with divine love, their souls illumine by the immaculate light, as Mary transforms them interiorly to do exactly what pleases God always. And for their reward, the Immaculate Heart of

Mary becomes a sure road, which opens up for the full communion of love among them all, as they are made brothers and sisters by the bond which unites them as children of one and the same Father, redeemed by one and the same Son, sanctified by one and the same Spirit, and become children of one sole Mother, the Virgin Mary.

Children of God, Mary is your true mother and so perfect a mother because she is the mother of Jesus. Through her we have received life in place of sin, immortality instead of mortality, light in place of darkness. She is indeed our mother, for through her we have been born, not for the world but for God. Whoever does not have Mary for his mother, does not have God for his father, and does not have Jesus Christ for his brother *1 Jn 2: 23*. The Protestants throw away this great Mother, the Son soon followed, and they are left with *temples of divine absence.*

"I thank You merciful Jesus, for having given us Mary as our Mother. And I thank You, Mary, for having given to the world the Divine Master, Jesus, who is the Way, the Truth, and the Life".

C H A P T E R 5

THE MARIAN CENACLE
THE APOSTLES PRAY WITH MARY

The surest way to obtain perfect sanctity, total transformation, and complete salvation from God is by way of the Most Blessed Virgin Mary. That is to say, by praying with Mary, in Mary, through Mary, by Mary, and for Mary. In *Acts 1: 14*, the apostles reunited themselves in prayer with Mary, waiting for the descent of the Holy Spirit. This gathering of prayer this best method of receiving the gifts of the Holy Spirit, is known as the *Cenacle* of prayer. This first one took place in the Upper Room, in Jerusalem, and so is referred to as the cenacle of Jerusalem. It is the liturgical time which occurs between the Solemnity of the Ascension and that of the Pentecost. A cenacle occurs whenever two or more persons unite themselves in prayer with Mary. She alone is the human agent and the Golden Door through which the Holy Spirit passes to come to us.

In this time we are living this time of civilization without

God this time of atheism, hedonism and egotism this time of evil and sin this wicked generation this predestined time this end of times this time of fake miracles and wonders this time of selling Jesus at a discount this time of Easter Sunday without Good Friday this time of cross less Christianity a time when the worship of God has become a matter of showbiz a time when the so called men and women of God merely resort to preaching the cross less Jesus this time when the enemy of the church is operating within the church this time when Pentecostalism has become the mode of worship within Catholicism a time when those Pentecostals within the church reunite themselves as a movement with the sole aim of destroying the Church, her traditions and our Blessed Mother, in pretext that they want to restructure, renew and modernize it - this time of wind of errors, great apostasy and the loss of the true faith this great hour of darkness, confusion, iniquity, and abomination in the holy sanctuary- this time when the presence of God is no longer acknowledged within the Church and respected by children of God a time when the answer to the problems created by false teachers within the church has become 'it does not matter'. Oh, this ugly time of great tribulations and chastisement, there is an urgent need for a Second Pentecost, that is to say, a total *renewal* and *transformation* of the whole world. This can only be possible by means of the powerful intercession of the Immaculate Heart of Mary, which is the new and spiritual cenacle of this end of times. The flames of the immaculate heart of Mary will always give us light on these days of darkness filled with heresies.

In the spiritual cenacle of the immaculate heart of Mary, everyone will be transformed and protected. This is evident in *Songs 4: 12 -13*. The Holy Spirit speaks of Mary in this form: *"My sweet heart, my spouse, is a secret garden, a walled garden: a private spring where the plants flourish and bear the finest fruit"*.

The Blessed Virgin Mary is the sweet heart and spouse of the Holy Spirit because Jesus Christ her son was conceived by the power of the Holy Spirit. The Holy Spirit has given Himself to Mary's soul by an interior and true spousal union, and of this union has been born the divine fruit of the virginal conception of the Word in her most pure womb. Therefore, she is the spouse of the Holy Spirit *Mt. 1: 20; Lk. 1: 35*. The *secret garden* symbolizes her immaculate heart where all the heavenly treasures are hidden. The *private spring* shows her as someone very special to God. It shows her as one who is privately and jealously chosen by God to become the source of life which is Jesus Christ. The *walled* or *fenced garden* shows Mary as the Defender and Protectress of the children of God, in both spiritual and physical warfare. It symbolizes the safe refuge of her immaculate heart with all the necessary weapons capable of defending and protecting the children of God, and to fight for them against the evil one and all his human agents. The *plants* that flourish in the garden of the immaculate heart of Mary represent all those who seek salvation from God as sons and daughters of Mary through whom they would bear the finest fruit which is

Jesus Christ.

In the spiritual cenacle of the immaculate heart of Mary, there will descend upon the Church and upon all humanity miraculous tongues of fire. The divine fire of love will enlighten and sanctify the Church which is living through the dark hour of Calvary, and being stricken in her pastors, wounded in the flock, abandoned and betrayed by her own, exposed to the impetuous wind of errors, pervaded with apostasy and the loss of the true faith. The Church will be healed of every sickness, purified of every stain and infidelity, clothed again in new beauty, and covered with the splendour of the Holy Spirit. And she will find again all her unity and holiness. Then she will give to the world her full universal and perfect witness to the gospel of Christ.

In the invocation of the gift of the Holy Spirit, let us always unite ourselves with the Virgin Mary, like the Apostles. The Holy Spirit cannot resist the voice of the spouse who calls to him. The more the Holy Spirit finds Mary, his dear and inseparable spouse in any soul, the more active and mighty he becomes in producing Jesus in that soul, and that soul in Jesus. The divine fire of love will burn away the sins which obscure the beauty of our souls. And we will return to the full communion of life with the heavenly Father; we will become a privileged garden, a wondrous garden, and a resplendent garden of God's divine presence; and in this beautiful garden there will blossom all the virtues cultivated with special care by the Virgin Mary, our heavenly Gardener.

In the end, the Holy Spirit will pour out his divine holiness upon the earth. And there will be a new miracle of universal transformation in the heart and life of all: sinners will be converted; the weak will be given support; the sick will receive healing; the gone astray will come back home; those separated and divided will attain full unity; and the whole world will become a new terrestrial paradise in which God Himself will be possessed, loved, lived, adored, and glorified by all and peace will be concealed to the human race. This way, the miracle of the Second Pentecost in union with the triumph of the Immaculate Heart of Mary will come to pass. This is a miracle of total transformation *Acts 2: 2 - 4.*

One thing that baffles me today is that even in the Catholic Church, of which Mary is the Mother, some people tend to separate her from the Holy Spirit. While some claim to belong to the Holy Spirit, others claim to belong to Mary. Children of God, Mary and the Holy Spirit are inseparably one *Songs 2: 16.* The Blessed Virgin is the spouse of the Holy Spirit. Therefore, what God has put together let no one put asunder *Mt. 19: 5 - 6; Mk. 10: 7 - 9.*

Finally, whoever does not have in him the Most Holy Mary also does not have in him the Holy Spirit of God, and so does not have in him the gifts of the Holy Spirit. No matter the miracles he performs, no matter the wonders, the truth is that he only camouflages and moves about in total emptiness, that is, in the emptiness of the grace of God.

C H A P T E R   6

MARY'S PERPETUAL VIRGINITY
ONLY JESUS IS BORN OF HER

When God created man, He made them man and woman-virgin Adam and virgin Eve-both of them full of grace. By disobedience, they betrayed God on the tree of paradise, they lost the grace of God and brought about the fall of the whole human race. But God in His infinite mercy decided to restore His grace in man. In order to do this, there was the need for a second Virgin Adam (Jesus Christ) and a second Virgin Eve (Virgin Mary). The will of God was that, since the fall of man was brought about by two individuals, man's restoration must be brought about by two individuals only. That is to say, by a woman and a man - Mary and Jesus - both of them full of grace - both of them perpetual virgins- **Gen. 3:15; Lk. 1:28; Jn. 1:14.**

Mary's purity of body and mind did not suffer any slightest stain of sin during her entire life. By an act of God, she enjoyed a unique and exclusive privilege of sublime sanctity. She was specially created by God to be the holiest sanctuary where He would dwell, and from whom He would assume human nature and be born into the world. For this reason, she was conceived and born immaculate, that is, without sin: that she might fit perfectly into the saving work of Christ. The Blessed Virgin had, from the onset, consecrated herself to God in virginity. She voluntarily and generously donated herself to God and lived in a state of total consecration to him. She mortified her senses and surrendered her human nature to the demands of divine grace. In an imperfect society of her time, she co-operated actively with the actions of the Holy Spirit to keep her vow of perpetual virginity and purity, despite obstacles and temptations. In all truth, Mary has lived a life of perpetual virginity.

In a bid to profane the honour due to Mary's perpetual virginity, non-Catholics (and even some Catholics) have clung to this portion of the Bible that says, *"And Mary gave birth to her first born"* Lk 2:7, to argue that she must have had other blood children after Jesus Christ. But *first-born* does not imply other children. It was a legal term for Jewish people: *the first-born was to be presented in the temple as Jesus was Ex 13:2; Lk 2:22*. The Blessed Virgin had no other blood children after Jesus Christ. But she has some other children according to the spirit. These are the Christians - the brothers and sisters of Jesus Christ-the spiritually adopted sons and daughters of God in *Gal. 4: 4- 5*. Now, let us visit the prophet Ezekiel and see what he has for us.

In the book of *Ezekiel 44:2-3* God says, *"This eastern gate of the temple shall remain closed, it shall never be opened. No human being is allowed to enter by this gate: for I, the Lord God of Israel, have entered by it. Therefore, it is to remain closed"*

My question: Is there any temple in Israel where no humanbeing is allowed to enter by the eastern gate?

My answer to this question is emphatic no. God is actually making a prophecy through the prophet Ezekiel about a living temple a temple that would come in human form a temple that would become the Ark of the New Covenant in which God Himself would actually dwell as a living Covenant. The Blessed Virgin is this temple. This prophecy was fulfilled in herself when she conceived in her virginal womb, Jesus the Saviour, who alone is the Lord God of Israel *Lk. 1: 26-38*. St. Elizabeth testified to this fact when she welcomed the Blessed Virgin as the Lord's Mother, that is, the Lord's Temple *Lk. 1: 43*. The eastern gate of the temple which has been perpetually closed by God, symbolizes Mary's perpetual virginity. Only Jesus Christ, the Lord God of Israel, had passed through her. Again, from Genesis to Revelation, only a woman and a seed (not many seeds) were mentioned by God *Gen 3:15; Isaiah 7:14; Rev. 12:5*. This goes to show that Mary had only one blood child, Jesus Christ.

In the Holy Bible, we will discover that all those who accuse Jesus of having blood brothers and sisters do not even know him, let alone knowing his brothers and sisters. This is evident in his question to his disciples: *"Who do people say I am?"* And they all replied: *"People say you are Elijah, John the*

Baptist or Jeremiah, or some other prophet of the old." These answers, apart from the one revealed by God to Peter, *"You are the Messiah, the Son of the living God" Mt. 16:13-17; Mk 8:27-30; Lk. 9:18-20,* prove that those people do not know Jesus neither do they know his father, nor his mother, his brothers nor his sisters, where he comes from nor where he would go to. Yes, because they all judge in a purely human form *Jn. 8:14 -15* and *19.* They do not know the degree of Mary's holiness. They do not know that she had taken the vow of perpetual virginity: that she would have nothing to do with sexual intercourse, let alone having blood children. This was even the reason while after receiving messages from the Angel, she questioned him and waited for his answer: that she might judge prudently whether the messages agreed with what the prophets had said about the Messiah, and with the principles of her religion *Lk. 1: 29 -30.* She wanted to know from the Angel whether the messages would mean forfeiting that vow of perpetual virginity, which she had made to God. When the Angel told her no, then, she knew it was authentic *Lk. 1:34 -35.* With the full consent of a full heart, full of God's love for her, and her own lowliness, she accepted the message: *"Behold, the handmaid of the Lord! Be it done unto me according to your word" Lk. 1:38.*

Brethren, Mary was only engaged in marriage to Joseph when she suddenly became pregnant *Lk. 1:27; Lk. 2:5* and they never had sexual relations, all through their life, since according to history and divine revelations, both of them had one same intention, that is, to remain perpetual virgins *Mt. 1:25.* The expression in some English translations regarding this particular portion of the Bible stating that Joseph *"had no marital relations with Mary until she had borne a son"*, seems to point to other children. This is because in English, the word *"UNTIL"* suggests that Joseph did have relations with Mary after the birth of Jesus. But *UNTIL* in the Greek or Aramaic (the original translations of the Bible), does not suggest that he did. It focuses only on the time up to the birth of Jesus, and says nothing about what happened thereafter. A similar expression in the book of Samuel states that Michal the daughter of Saul *"had no child to the day of her death"* 2 Sam. 6:23. Here the English translation uses *"To"* instead of *"UNTIL"* but the original word behind both phrases is the same, and obviously Michal did not have children after her death. In *Matt. 28:20* Jesus says, *"I am with you always, to the end of the age."* The word translated here as *"To"* is the same as the *"UNTIL"* of *Mt.1:25*. Here, Jesus obviously means that he will be with his disciples you and me, until the end of the world and beyond the end of the world, that is, forever. In the same way, *Mt. 1:25* can carry the meaning that Joseph had no marital relations with Mary until and beyond the time she gave birth to Jesus. This was the reason for Joseph's confusion that he almost broke off the engagement *Mt. 1:19*. He knew he had not done anything sexual with Mary, as to warrant her pregnancy neither would he do so afterwards, so as to keep his vow. But he did not know that although God could still have allowed her to have her baby outside marriage, He preferred to use him to safeguard the pregnancy so that people would not stone her to death, thinking that she had committed adultery which is an abomination in both the Jewish culture and the worship of

God *Jn 8:3-5*. Again, God did not want Jesus to appear to the people as a bastard. Hence, he chose Joseph to be his *foster father*. To clear Joseph's confusion, God sent his Angel to explain to him (and in a sense, to all of us) that Mary's virginal pregnancy was by means of the power of the Holy Spirit, so as to make Isaiah's prophecy come true: *"that a virgin shall conceive and bear a son and shall call his name Immanuel"* Isaiah 7:14; Mt. 1:20-23. By this fact, it became clearer all the more to him that both of them were still faithful to each other's vow, that is, the vow of perpetual virginity. They now witnessed the miracle of Jesus' conception and birth, and realized that God had entrusted them the greatest treasure in the history of the world, His only begotten son. They understood their task in life was to nurture and protect the Saviour of the human race.

Many years later, Jesus would speak of those who renounced marriage *"for the sake of the kingdom of heaven"* Mt. 19:12. So, it cannot be surprising that Mary and Joseph would have given up their right to have other children in order to dedicate their lives exclusively to the care of the Son of God. The fact that Jesus was Mary's only blood child underlines his uniqueness as the only Son of God. These facts, rooted in the Bible and clarified by the Church's tradition, help us to see Jesus in the clearest possible light. And since the Church is guided by the Holy Spirit, we can be certain that the Church's belief in Mary's perpetual virginity has been inspired by the Holy Spirit.

In the Old Testament, God had manifested Himself in so many ways to explain to the world that his Blessed Mother would remain forever a virgin. Therefore, she would have nothing to do with having many blood children other than Jesus Christ. In the book of *Exodus 3:2-6*, God appeared to Moses on Mount Sinai, as a flame coming from the middle of the bush. The bush was on fire but was not burning up.

Children of God, the image of the un-burnt bush symbolizes Mary's perpetual virginity, whereas the fire itself symbolizes Jesus in the womb of Mary, that is, the *Divine Fire of the Incarnate Word contained in the Virginal Chamber of the heavenly Queen*. That is to say, Mary had conceived and given birth to Jesus, yet she did not loose her virginity hence we call her *'Virgin Mother'*. Some revelations have it that Mary did not give birth to Jesus in the same manner as other women do. Rather, it was by means of her right side. Yes, otherwise she would not have remained a virgin till date. This cannot be surprising in that, if Jesus could enter and leave the room where his disciples gathered to pray, without necessarily opening the door and passing through it *Jn. 20:19-20*, what prevents him then from entering and leaving his most holy city his holiest sanctuary his most holy tabernacle the most pure womb of Mary, without necessarily making her to loose her virginity? Jesus is God and there is nothing impossible for him to do *Mk 10:27; Lk1:37*.

If Jesus really had some actual brothers and sisters, where were they when he handed his mother over to John, the son of Zebedee? *Jn 19:26 27*. His action would have made no sense. Perhaps there was enmity between him and members of his family. In all truth, all those whom the Bible refers to as brothers and sisters of Christ in *Mt. 13:55-56; Mk. 3:31 35; Lk 8:19-20; Jn. 2:12; Jn. 7:3; Acts 1:14,* are not related to him according to the flesh. But because these people, together with all true Christians, the disciples of Christ, you and me, obey the commandment of God, Jesus calls them his brothers and sisters *Mt. 12: 46-50; Lk 8:21.*

Amongst the Disciples of Christ some were related to him and his mother Mary in a special way, but not as sons and daughters of Mary according to the flesh. This relationship has to do with the genealogy, birth, and marriage of St. Anne, the mother of the Virgin Mary. The Ancestors of Anne were Essenians. They were extra-ordinarily pious people. They descended from those priests who carried the Ark in the time of Moses and Aaron, and who received precise rules in the days of Isaiah and Jeremiah. They migrated from Palestine to the region of the Jordan where they dwelt chiefly on Mount Horeb and Mount Carmel.

In early times the Essenians lived scattered as pious, ascetic Jews before they were gathered together by Isaiah. They neither changed nor repaired their garments until they actually fell to pieces. They married but observed great continence in the married state. With mutual consent husband and wife frequently lived apart in distant huts. They also ate apart, first the husband and on his departure the wife. Even in those early times some of the fore fathers of St. Anne and other members of the Holy Family were found among them. From them sprang those that are called the children of the Prophets. They dwelt in the desert and around Mount Horeb.

At the time of Anne's grandparents was the Superior, a prophet named Archos. He had visions in the cave of Elijah on Horeb, referring to the coming of the Messiah. He knew from what family the Messiah would come and, when he prophesied to Anne's grandparents concerning their posterity, he saw that the time was drawing near. But since he did not know exactly how far it would be or how it might still be delayed by sin, he exhorted to penance and sacrifice.

Anne's grandfather, *Stolanus*, was an Essenian. He was called by the name Garescha or Sarziri by his wife, *Emorun* and in consideration of her dowry. She was of Mara in the desert. Her name Moruni, or Emorun signifies noble mother. She married Stolanus upon the advice of the prophet Archos, who was the Superior of the Essenians for ninety years. Archos was a very holy man with whom counsel was always taken by those intending to enter upon the married state, that they might make a good choice.

If the Superior prayed concerning a marriage, he took the staff of Aaron into his hand. If the union in question would contribute to Mary's lineage, the staff put forth a bud from which sprang one or more blossoms bearing the sign of the choice. The forefathers of Anne were legitimate descendants of this lineage, and their chosen daughters had been by such signs designated. New blossoms burst forth whenever a chosen daughter was to enter the married state. The little tree with its spiral leaves was like a genealogical table, like the root of Jesse, and by it could be seen how far the advent of the Virgin Mary was distant.

When *Stolanus* got married to *Emorun,* they had their daughters: *Emerentia, Ismeria, and Enue.* Emerentia grew up, got married to a Levite named *Aphras,* and became the mother of *Elizabeth* (who became the mother of John the Baptist). Ismeria grew up and got married to *Eliud,* of the tribe of Levi and became the mother of *Sobe, Anne,* and *Maraha.* Anne was not born until 18years after the birth of her eldest sister, Sobe. In *Lk. 1:36,* Angel Gabriel addresses Elizabeth as Virgin Mary's sister. This is because Elizabeth's mother who is *Emerentia* and Mary's grandmother who is *Ismeria* are biological sisters. By extension, *John the Baptist* could be called Jesus' brother. For while *Emerentia* is his grandmother, *Ismeria* is Jesus' great grandmother.

Sobe got married to Solomon and became the mother of *Mary Salome.* Mary Salome got married to *Zebedee* and became the mother of the future apostles: *James* (the Greater) and *John* (the Beloved)*Mt.20:20; Mk.10:35.*

One night before St. Anne was born, both father (Eliud) and mother (Ismeria) had the same vision upon their couch. Ismeria saw an Angel near her writing on the wall. On awakening she told her husband who also had the same vision. They saw the written character on the wall. It was the letter 'M' symbolizing Mary, an indication that the yet to be born daughter, Anne, would become the mother of the Virgin Mary.

Since the ancestors of Anne descended from those priests that carried the Ark in the time of Moses and Aaron, it became necessary that by the means of this vision God reassured her parents that the Ark which in the New Testament is the Virgin Mary, who is of better quality than the Ark of Old, would still be within their lineage. At the birth of Anne, she brought with her into the world the same sign (the letter 'M') upon the region of the stomach.

Anne found in her paternal house a little son of her eldest sister. The boy's name was Eliud (the same name as Anne's father). Afterward Anne's youngest sister, Maraha, inherited the paternal property of *Sephoris* and became the mother of the subsequent disciples, *Arastaria* and *Cocharia*. The young Eliud afterward became the second husband of *Maroni*, of Naim.

Anne married *Joachim Heli,*of the House of David, for the Virgin Mary was to belong to the House of David; otherwise she (Anne) would have had to choose her husband from among the Levites of the tribe of Aaron, as all her race had done. She had had many suitors and, yet acquainted with Joachim. She chose him only upon supernatural direction.

Joachim was a relative of *St. Joseph* whose grandfather, *Mathan* had descended from David through Solomon. Mathan had two sons, *Joses* and *Jacob*. The later became the father of St. Joseph (the foster father of Jesus the Saviour). When Mathan died, his widow married a second husband, *Levi*, descendant of David through Nathan. The fruit of this marriage was Mathat, the father of Joachim. By this account we could see that Joachim was a relative of St. Joseph because his father (Mathat) and Joseph's father (Jacob) were of the same mother (but not of the same father).

When Anne married Joachim, they had a daughter, *Mary Heli*. Anne became barren for 20years before having a second daughter, the *Blessed Virgin Mary* (the mother of Jesus the Saviour). The reason why *James* and *John* were called brothers of Jesus is because, *Sobe*, who was their grandmother and *Anne*, who was Jesus' grandmother were biological sisters. *Mary Heli* got married to *Clopas*, and they had a daughter named *Mary Jn. 19:25*. This one was named after her mother because the Jews like repeating names within the family *Lk. 1:61*. *Mary Clopas* now married *Alphaeus* (the brother of Joseph the husband of Mary), and they had *Jude Thaddaeus, Simon* (the Zealot) and *James* (the least) *Mk 3:18*. *James* the least looked so much like Jesus that people thought he was Virgin Mary's blood child and they referred to him as the *Lord's brother*. These three Apostles were called brothers of Jesus Christ because *Mary Heli*, who was their grandmother, was Virgin Mary's elder sister. It is important to note that before marrying Mary *Clopas*, *Alphaeus* had previously married a woman who bore him a male child before she died. That male child was *Mathew the tax collector*. This goes to show that *Mathew* and the other sons of *Alphaeus* were step brothers (the name Mathew has ancient

Hebrew origins meaning *"gift of Yahweh")*.

Brethren, we have now seen that these people mentioned so far were not of the same mother with Jesus Christ. Rather, they only related to him and his Mother Mary. They are the relatives of Jesus and Mary. Moreover, in both Biblical and Jewish terms, *"brothers and sisters"* might refer to members of the same tribe, or nieces, or nephews, or kinsmen and kinswomen respectively, or cousins, or relatives in general *Gen. 13:8; Gen. 29:15; Deut. 15:12; Deut. 23:7; 2Kings 10:13; 1 Chro.23:22; Lev.10:4.* It is this type of relationship that existed between Jesus and those whom people referred to as his brothers and sisters. The New Testament never speaks of other children of Mary or Joseph. So, it is impossible to prove from the Bible that Jesus actually had blood brothers or sisters. The Most Holy Mary remained a virgin, in heart and in body, before giving birth to Jesus, in giving birth to Jesus, and after having given birth to Jesus. She conceived virginally, gave birth virginally, and remained an undefiled virgin unto death. She was pure in heart and deed. She was most pure, most chaste, inviolate and undefiled. Her fullness of innocence is therefore, next to God.

In all truth, Jesus had no actual blood brothers or sisters. Rather, those who follow his way he has made to become his brothers and sisters *Jn. 20:17-18.* .

My dear brothers and sisters, from what we have learned so far, you can agree with me that Mary had no other blood children after Jesus Christ. Therefore, anyone who continues to preach that Jesus had some actual blood brothers and sisters is only blaspheming against Jesus and his blessed Mother. And the punishment due to the sin of blasphemy is eternal death, *an everlasting banishment in hell fire* Heb. 10:28-30; 1 Tim. 1:20. These beliefs, old as the New Testament and new as today, it is my prayer, should enrich your lives and those of countless generations to come.

C H A P T E R   7

MARY
THE SECOND EVE
GEN. 3:15

After the victory of Satan on the tree of paradise, in the fall of man through Adam and Eve, God became angry and said to him: *"I will put enmity between you and the woman, between your seed and her seed: she will crush your head and you will bite her heel"* - Gen. 3:15. Many people do not know the woman God was actually talking about here, to crush the head of Satan. While some claim it is Eve, others maintain that it is the Virgin Mary. But in order for us to really understand this prophecy and choose between these two, Eve and Mary, who precisely the Bible is talking about, we must begin by tracing their roles, their offspring, their office and position, as well as their relationship with God and Satan. This is due to the fact that the enmity as decreed by God, is also extended to all these.

In the book of *Gen. 3:6*, Eve disobeyed God by listening to Satan and eating the forbidden fruit. This way, she obeyed

Satan and he became her master. Then, in *verse 20*, the Bible says that the seed of Eve is *all men*, that is, the entire human race, whereas in *Jn. 8:44*, the Bible says that *sin* is the seed of Satan. Then, in *Rm. 3:23*, the Bible says that all men have sinned and fallen short of God's grace.

Now, since Eve has obeyed Satan and her seed also, that is all men, obeyed the seed of Satan which is sin, it means there is no enmity between Eve and Satan, and between the seed of Eve and the seed of Satan, rather they have all become friends. They have all become friends because Satan himself has now become their master. Satan has become their master because they have all obeyed him, and a person automatically becomes a servant or slave of the master that he obeys *Rm. 6:16*. By disobedience, Eve has destroyed all her children (you and me) together with herself, and has delivered them to her master, the red dragon. This is to show that Eve is not the woman promised by God to crush the head of Satan in *Gen. 3:15*. Instead, she is that woman whom Satan himself has crushed her head, together with all her children.

Children of God, since it was due to the disobedience of the first woman, Eve, that all men became sinners, it became necessary that all men would become righteous due to the obedience of a second woman *Rm. 5:18-19*. That is to say, since man has lost the grace of God, and so lost his way to heaven because of the disobedience of the first woman, Eve, it became necessary that man should regain the lost grace, and so find his way to heaven because of the obedience of a second woman. When this is done, the second woman would have crushed the head of Satan to pieces.

In *Lk. 1:26 38*, the Virgin Mary obeyed God by listening to his Angel, receiving and accepting his message of salvation, and putting it into practice. This way, God became her master *Lk. 1:38*.

The seed of Mary is Jesus Christ *Mt. 1:18; Lk. 2:34*, while the seed of Satan is sin *Jn. 8:44*. In *Jn. 1:29*, the Bible says that Jesus came into the world to fight against sin and destroy it. Now, since the Virgin Mary did not obey Satan, but God, and her seed also, that is, Jesus Christ, came into the world to fight against sin the seed of Satan, it means there is enmity between the Virgin Mary and Satan, and between the seed of the Virgin Mary and the seed of Satan. No wonder, whenever the Blessed Virgin comes one on one with Satan, war breaks out *Rev. 12:13-17*. This implies that the Virgin Mary is the second woman promised by God, and prophesied about in the Bible to crush the head of Satan in *Gen. 3: 15*. By bruising or biting the heel of Mary, the serpent wages great battle against the children of God and Mary who are symbolized as the heel of Mary in *Rev.12:17*. This great battle, this incomprehensible enmity, is not just an enmity, but enmities, not simply between the Blessed Virgin and Satan, but also, between the true children and servants of Mary and the children and servants of Satan. This is an irreconcilable enmity, which must grow and endure to the end of the world.

And since, as decreed by God, it is between two principal actors, namely:

(1)   The Blessed Virgin, for all forces of good and for the glory of God,

(2)   The Dragon, for all forces of evil and for the glory of Satan,

it implies that God has given to mankind only two options from which to make a choice of whom they belong to. Therefore, anyone who is not on the side of Mary is on the side of Satan. Anyone who is not in the party or army or legion of Mary, is clearly in the legion of Satan. Anyone who does not declare for the Virgin Mary automatically declares for Satan. Anyone who does not believe in the Mother of Christ is clearly a believer in Satan. If you (the reader) belong to the Holy Mother of God, then, you belong to God and to all forces of good. But if you do not belong to Mary, the truth is that you belong to Satan and to all forces of evil. It is either you are here or you are there. You either belong to the Virgin Mary or you belong to Satan. You must belong somewhere. There is no neutral ground. What I have said so far, I have no apology to anyone.

Those who belong to the party of the Blessed Virgin (of which I am a proud and perpetual member), are the people with whom the most powerful Virgin fight for the truth, for God, and for the good of all his church. These are the people who in imitation of Jesus Christ, honour the heavenly Queen in spirit and in truth. These people go about proclaiming the glory of the worthy mother of salvation.

Those who belong to the party of Satan are the people with whom the red dragon, fight against Mary, the church and her tradition. These are the human agents of Satan who insult our Most Heavenly Empress, blaspheme her most holy name by calling her an envelope, queen of the coast, an ordinary woman, a goddess or a carved image. They also attack her beloved children, calling them idol worshippers. Oh, the heat is on. The stage is set. The battle line is drawn. It is going to be very explosive, and we shall all fight this battle to the end. One thing is certain; the victory belongs to Jesus and Mary, and to all sons and daughters of God and Mary. After running the race, we count the mileage.

Brethren, it is very painful, very sorrowful, and very agonizing, that a thing like this continues to happen in the world today. Whenever you see or hear anyone refusing to honour the Blessed Virgin and heaping insults on her, know you that it is in fulfillment of *Gen. 3:15*. But remember, the increased efforts of the forces of evil in this end of times, can only be countered by a corresponding increase of devotion to the Most Blessed Virgin.

Children of God, by obedience, the Blessed Virgin has saved all her children, the Christians, together with herself *1Tim. 2:15*. She has liberated them, snatched them away from Satan, and consecrated and delivered them to their master, the God Almighty. Yes, God is said to be their master because they obey him. And a person automatically becomes a servant of the master that he obeys *Rm. 6:16.*

Some other facts that confirm the Blessed Virgin as the second woman promised by God to crush the head of Satan are these: While the first woman, Eve, was made a helpmate to the first man, Adam *Gen. 2:18-21*, the Blessed Virgin was also made a helpmate to the second man, Christ Jesus *Jer. 31:22.* To buttress this fact, Simeon said to Mary, *"And sorrow, like a sharp sword, will break your own heart" Lk. 2:35.* That is to say, she has been chosen by God to share in a special way, the sufferings involved in the saving work of Christ. In other words, she has been chosen as a helpmate to Jesus in correcting the wrong of Adam and Eve. This way, the Blessed Virgin became the second Eve, while Jesus Christ became the second Adam *1 Cor. 15:45 49; Rm. 5:12-15.*

Again, in the same way as the first Adam offered thanksgiving to God because he and the first Eve were of the same blood, flesh and bone, so did Jesus Christ the second Adam, offer thanksgiving to God in the New Testament because he and Mary, the second Eve, were of the same blood, flesh and bone *Gen. 2:21 23; Heb 10:5.*

Again, while Eve wrongly advised Adam to disobey God *Gen 3: 6 - 7*, the Blessed Virgin correctly advised Jesus to do the will of God. Firstly, she made him remain obedient to her *Lk. 2:48 51.* Secondly, she advised him to attend to the need of the people by turning water into wine *Jn. 2:1-11.* All these testify to the fact that Jesus also obeys that same commandment of God that says, *"Obey your father and your mother" Ex. 20:12; Sir. 3:3-6.* It is not that Jesus was ignorant of all these, rather he only wanted Mary to play the role of the second Eve.

And just as in the sleep of the first Adam, his right side was made open and from there came forth the first Eve, so also, in the sleep of Jesus Christ on the cross of Calvary, his right side was made open by the lance, and from there came forth the Church, the new Eve, the new Mother of the living. And while because of Eve all men became sinners, so also, by means of the blood and water, which came forth from the right side of Jesus, we all have been washed and cleansed of this original sin, to become righteous-*Jn. 19:34.*

According to history and divine revelations, when Adam and Eve were driven out of the Garden of Eden, Adam took some plants along with him which he planted in their new place of settlement. One of these plants was the olive. And out of this olive tree was made the cross of Jesus Christ. It was also revealed that in the Old Israel, one of the disciples of the Great Elijah, found a human skull on Mount Calvary, and in trying to remove the skull, an angel appeared to him and warned him not to do so, *"For that was the skull of Adam".* Since then, that place has been called the *'place of the skull'* or the *'Golgotha'* in the Jewish language. It was on this same spot that the holy cross of Jesus Christ was mounted so that, where the first Adam died, Jesus the second Adam would also die *Mt. 27:33 35; Mk. 15:22 25; Jn. 19:17 18.*

The plan of God was not for Jesus to do the work of Eve; rather he wanted him to do the work of the second Adam. Adam introduced sin into the world, but this was through the first woman, Eve. He was not the person that actually sinned, since he did not meet with Satan one on one. Rather, Eve was the person that actually sinned for she was the one that met with Satan one on one *1 Tim. 2:14.* The reason why Adam is referred to as the person that introduced sin into the world is because though Eve was the one that actually sinned, she made Adam to sin also, by offering him the forbidden fruit, and the fate of the human race lay with Adam. If Adam had not fallen, if he had stood his ground, we would not have lost those supernatural privileges. He was the one that represented us. It was in him that we fell. For he was the one upon whom those privileges, were bestowed. He was our first father and the head of the human race.

On the other hand, Eve had a definite, essential position in the First Covenant. For although she was not the head of the human race, yet even as regards the race she had a place of her own. For Adam who was divinely commissioned with the naming of all things named her 'the mother of all the living'. By virtue of this name, she had her own general relation to the human race, as well as her own special place in its trial and fall in Adam. She was the one that originally started the fall of man: for she co-operated not as an irresponsible instrument, but intimately and personally in the sin. She brought it about. She was a *sine- qua-non: a positive active cause of it.* And she had her share in its punishment. In the sentence pronounced on her, she was recognized as a real agent in the temptation and its issue, and so she suffered accordingly.

Now, by the position and office of Eve in the fall of man, we can determine the position and office of the Blessed Virgin in our restoration. So, since Eve was the one that had a direct contact with Satan, it became necessary that God would pronounce a direct enmity between Mary (the second Eve) and Satan, while Jesus Christ (the second Adam) would be responsible in taking away from the world, the seed of Satan which is sin, which was introduced by the first Adam *Jn. 1:29.*

In the Garden of Gethsemane, Jesus began his agony at the exact spot grotto where Adam and Eve had landed, after they were driven from Paradise. On this same spot, they fell down and atoned for their sin. So, it also became necessary that Jesus the second Adam would begin his agony and atonement on the same spot-*Lk.22:39-44.*

The Garden of Gethsemane was a place of numerous atrocities. It was there that Abel was murdered by his brother, Cain-*Gen. 4:8-11.* When some ancient Jews fell into idolatry, they sacrificed within the same area. Jesus atoned for all these. The bloody sweat that dropped to the ground during his agony was meant to atone partly for the defilement caused by the blood of Abel which was spilled by Cain.

Satan used three instruments in the fall of man: *Eve the first woman, Adam the first man, and the tree of paradise.* Therefore, it became necessary that God would also use three instruments in our restoration: *the Blessed Virgin the second woman, Christ Jesus the second man, and the tree of Calvary,* which is the cross. These instruments used by God are called the *"three major instruments of salvation."* Thus, for anyone to attain complete salvation, he must embrace these three instruments, that is, the Blessed Virgin, Jesus Christ and the Cross. Otherwise, he experiences an incomplete salvation. God has wanted that just as Eve and Adam (lost his divine grace and) destroyed man on the tree of paradise, Mary and Jesus (who are the only ones full of God's grace*Lk.1:28;Jn.1:14*) would redeem man on the tree of Calvary; *that the tree of man's defeat would become his tree of victory: where life was lost, there life would be restored Jn. 19:28-30; Col. 2:14-15.*

Eve was still a virgin when she received and believed the message of eternal death from the angel of darkness while the blessed Mary also as a virgin (and forever a virgin), received and believed the message of eternal life from the angel of light. In other words, while the virgin Eve listened to the angel of darkness, the Virgin Mary listened to the angel of light. By a virgin, the human race had been bound to death, yet by a virgin it is saved: *that of the virgin Eve the Virgin Mary might become the advocate.*

The blessed Virgin was not a mere instrument in the Incarnation. She co-operated in our salvation not merely by the descent of the Holy Spirit upon her body, rather by specific holy acts, the effect of the Holy Spirit within her soul. She was an intelligent, responsible cause of it due to her faith and obedience, the virtues of which Eve has failed. As Eve made room for the fall of Adam, the Virgin Mary made room for Christ's reparation of it. And since the *free gift* was not as the *offence* but much greater *Rm. 5:15 - 17*, it follows that as the virgin Eve co-operated in effecting a great evil, the Virgin Mary co-operated in effecting a much greater good. So, by a rival operation God has now recovered his image and likeness which had been seized by Satan. What Eve has damned and lost by disobedience, the Blessed Virgin has gained and saved by obedience. She has repaired Eve's disobedience and become her advocate and that of the entire human race. She alone has given the miserable children of Eve *(you and me)*, entry into the kingdom of heaven. She has therefore, merited everything for us. She has made it possible that we the poor banished children of Eve have been saved, to become sons and daughters of God. This is what we call the *"Total Restoration."* She will continue to bring souls into heaven until she fills with many great saints, the empty thrones from which Lucifer and his fallen angels were dethroned and driven away *Rev.12:7 - 9*.

Brethren, we are no longer the children of Eve *(the woman short of grace)*. For she has been deprived of this privilege and banished by God, together with all her children *Gen. 3:20-23.* This is the reason why we invoke the Blessed Virgin in the prayer of the Hail Holy Queen, saying, *"To you do we cry, poor banished children of Eve; to you do we send up our sighs, mourning and weeping in this valley of tears..."* And as we are no longer the children of Eve, we have all become the adopted sons and daughters of Mary as St. Paul testifies: *"Send the slave - woman and her son (or children) away; for the son of the slave woman will not have a part of the father's property along with the son of the free woman. So then, my brothers, we are no longer the children of the slave woman but of the free woman"* *Gal 4: 30 - 31.* These two women: the slave woman and the free woman, are figures representing two other women. While the slave woman symbolizes Eve, the free woman symbolizes Virgin Mary. Yes, because by disobedience, Eve has lost the grace of God and has become a slave of Satan and the mother of all the dying. While the Blessed Virgin, by obedience, retains her fullness of grace and so remains a free woman and the new and everlasting mother of all the living. It is the children of Mary the redeemed man the adopted sons and daughters of God you and me in *Gal. 4:4-5*, that will partake in the father's property which is life everlasting in heaven, along with Jesus Christ the Son of Mary *(the free woman)* *Rev. 12:17.* This gives significance to the statement made by Jesus on the cross with regard to Mary, *"Woman, behold your son, son, behold* your mother," that is to say, "Blessed Virgin, redeemed man is your children, redeemed man, Blessed Virgin is your mother" Jn 19:26-27. This implies that anyone who does not accept and acknowledge Mary as his salvific mother also does not want to enter into the kingdom of heaven. On the last day, in the same way as Jesus says, "Father, all the people you gave to me, I have protected them: not even one of them was lost by me, except the man who was bound to be lost," so shall the Blessed Virgin say, "My Lord and my Son, Christ Jesus, all those you gave to me at the foot of the cross to become my children, I have protected them: not even one of them was lost by me, except the man who separated himself from my children" - Jn. 17:12.

Children of God do not be afraid of Satan. Stand firm in the Blessed Virgin Mary. Anyone who stands firm in Mary will always be capable of crushing the head of Satan because Mary herself, who is constantly by your side, has already crushed the head of Satan to pieces. She will always crush the head of Satan because she is full of grace and possesses the power and wisdom of God Lk. 1:28; Wis. 7:25. God Himself has made her all - powerful, by way of the *Trinitarian Abidingness* and *Indwelling*, that is to say, she is full of power and glory of the Most Blessed Trinity. She is in the Trinity because Jesus Christ the fruit of her womb is in the Trinity.

She is full of power and glory of God the Father because she is the Daughter of the Father. She is full of power and glory of God the Son because she is the Mother of God the Son. She is full of power and glory of God the Holy Spirit because she is the Spouse of the Holy Spirit. This is what we call the *"Trinitarian Empowerment."*

In summary, Mary has crushed the head of Satan by her obedience to God. She therefore, obtains peace for mankind, glory for the heavens, salvation for the lost, life for the dead, the union of God Himself with mankind, and a heavenly parentage for the human race.

C H A P T E R 8

MARY
THE COMMANDER IN CHIEF OF THE ROYAL ARMED FORCES OF GOD (SONGS 6:10)

In the Old Testament, some people were privileged to receive revelations from God regarding his promise of salvation to the human family. In one of these mysterious revelations, king Solomon was privileged to see the woman chosen by God from the beginning (though yet to be born), as the most appropriate and a most genuine means to bring his divine promise to fulfillment. To this effect, the Blessed Virgin appears to be the woman chosen by God the woman of *Gen.3:15*, the Conquest of Satan and Rescue to man. She appears as a great Army Leader, the Commander in Chief of the Royal Armed Forces of God, moving victoriously to battle against the enemy of our salvation that ancient serpent called Satan or the red dragon. In *Song of Songs 6:10*, a revelation of the Virgin Mary was made to Solomon, and because she appeared as an army leader, moving confidently in her royal majesty, in perfect beauty, glory and splendour, and in great power, Solomon was moved to ask, *"Who is this woman that cometh forth as the Morning Rising: fair as the Moon: bright as the Sun: terrible as an Army set in battle array?"* God uses this great revelation to strengthen Solomon's faith in Him and hope in His promise of salvation, giving him to understand that time was fast approaching for the restoration of the fallen human race.

In this great revelation, the Blessed Virgin is described as the *Moon*. She is said to be the *Moon* because according to St. Alphonsus De Liguori, in the same way as the moon gives light in the darkness of the night, so does she give light in the darkness of our souls that darkness which is found in the hearts of people the spiritual darkness. This is the miserable state of sinfulness in which so many people are living their lives today that state of sinfulness which began with the first woman, Eve, and spread to the whole of human race. When Mary the second woman enters into our lives as the *Moon,* in her graciousness, she enlightens those who wander blindly in the night of sin. With the flames of her immaculate heart, she helps them to see and understand the miserable state of damnation in which they are so that they may come out from it and do not die eternally.

Again, the Bible describes the Blessed Virgin as the Morning Rising *(i.e. the Dawn).* And since it is after the dawn, that early morning hour, comes the rising Sun, it implies that she is the *Fore Runner* of the Sun to the people of God, especially those whom she has already enlightened and made to renounce sin, and return once again to the true God, who Himself is the true Sun of justice so that when it shines on them, no stain of sin will be found.

Again, the Blessed Virgin is said to be as bright as the Sun. This brightness of the Sun symbolizes her 'Immaculateness', that is, the high degree of Mary's holiness and purity. She is the Sun so that she might illuminate with the light of her immaculate heart those who are in a state of divine grace and prevent them from falling again into sin.

Finally, the Bible says that Mary is as terrible as an army set in battle array, that is, the battle to crush the head of Satan the battle against heresy, apostasy and bad doctrine the battle of victory of good over every form of evil and sin the battle to do the will of God the battle to sustain the faith of the church and her children you and me in Christ. The Blessed Virgin is indeed, a great fighter, a Great War Leader, capable of leading the children of God to victory over the red dragon and his human agents. The word 'Army' as used in the context symbolizes the soldiers of Mary her victorious cohort the legion of Mary. These are all soldiers of God, greatly empowered by Him, and marching on to victory, in confidence and fearlessness, beneath the standard of Mary, the Virgin most powerful. This Marian Army is divided into three groups. The first group is made up of all the people that form the Church of Christ in heaven. The second group is made up of all the people that form the Church of Christ in purgatory. The third and final group includes all the people that form the Church of Christ which is in this world. The Church of Christ in heaven is made up of all the people who have been washed in the blood of the lamb. They have run their heavenly race faithfully. They have fought the battle and won the victory. They are now wearing their glorious crowns of victory, rejoicing in the everlasting happiness of heaven with Jesus Christ, the Blessed Virgin, the Angels of God and Saints in heaven. This one is what we call the *"Triumphant Church"* Rev. 7: 9-17. The Church of Christ which is in purgatory is made up of all the people who have passed away from this world, but have not entered into heaven, yet they are not in hell. These include all the people whose sins have been forgiven, but were not fully expiated by them or reparated for, while on earth. This is a spiritual condition in which the soul is purified by temporal punishment in preparation for heaven. This one is what we call the *"Suffering Church."* The Church of Christ which is in this world is the Holy Roman Catholic and Apostolic Church which is in great battle with Satan. This one is what we call the *"Militant Church."* In the Catholic Church, the soldiers of Mary in a special way include members of the following pious societies, namely: the Legion of Mary, the Blue Army, the Block Rosary, the Marian Movement, the Rosa Mystica and other different groups in the church.

In this great battle, all children of God must fight beneath the standard of Mary. This explains the reason why in the Catena prayer we say to Jesus: *"Confer O Lord on us, who serve beneath the standard of Mary, that fullness of faith in you and trust in her, to which it is given to conquer the world."* In all truth, in this end of times, the attack of the forces of evil against the children of Mary is on the increase. Only those who shall remain faithful to the end, no matter the obstacles, shall win the battle with Mary. They will be glorified by God, the Blessed Virgin, the Angels of God and Saints in heaven. Their crown is assured in heaven. While on earth, the Queen of heaven continues to fight for them. She holds them in high esteem and testifies to their words that they are truly her own. Now let us visit the book of Revelation, chapter twelve *the woman and the dragon.*

THE WOMAN AND THE DRAGON:
THE INTERPRETATION OF REV. 12

In the book of Revelation, chapter twelve, we come to the fulfillment of the promise and prophecy of God in *Gen. 3:15*. In this passage of the Bible, we shall see clearly how the Blessed Virgin and Satan fought that great battle. It shows how the Most Powerful Virgin scourges the red dragon, the enemy of our salvation. It shows how she punishes him, defeats him, and crushes his head to pieces, then restores the glory and victory of God to man.

In this mysterious event, Satan appears in the form of a huge red dragon, with seven heads and ten horns, with a crown on each of its heads. While the Blessed Virgin clothed with the sun, with a crown of twelve stars on her head, and the moon under her feet, appears as an **a**ction-woman, that same great woman revealed to King Solomon in the Old Testament. Now let us go straight - away into the activities of these two great enemies, the Blessed Virgin and Satan - the woman and the dragon.

About The Dragon
In the activities of Satan, the *"Huge Red Dragon"* symbolizes a government which does not acknowledge the existence of God. It is called the *"Atheistic Communism."* It is a bad government which originated from Russia, a Communist Country, and goes about in the world spreading its error of the denial and rejection of God because of its knowledge of

science and technology. This is a government that was founded by a Russian Atheist known as Marxy and so it is referred to as the *'Marxist Atheism.'* The word atheism is derived from the Greek *atheos*, which means *"without a god."* An atheist is a person who practices atheism, that is, he does not believe in the reality of God. This explains the reason why the Blessed Virgin requested at Fatima, the prayers for the conversion of Russia and its consecration by the church to her immaculate heart.

The *'Hugeness'* of the dragon stands for the volume of the territory occupied by the atheistic communism or government.

The *'Ten Horns'* of the dragon stand for its power and means of communication with which it leads humanity to disobey the ten (10) commandments of God.

The *'Red Colour'* of the dragon stands for its instruments of attack, that is, war and blood.

The *'Crowned Heads'* of the dragon stand for all the nations in which atheism is ideologically, politically and militarily established in the world today.

About Virgin Mary. The Blessed Virgin appears clearly in the sky as a woman with incomparable beauty, possessing the light of God, power and wisdom with which to fight the red dragon to submission.

The 'Crown' on the head of Mary is a sign of royalty. It confirms that she is a Queen that great Queen whom God had spoken about in heaven. The crown is made up of twelve (12) stars because it is a symbol of Mary's maternal and royal presence in the very hearts of the people of God.

The 'Twelve Stars' around the crown stand for the twelve tribes of Israel, the twelve Apostles upon whom Jesus Christ founded the Catholic Church, the Reverend Fathers, and all persons who accept the Blessed Virgin as their Mother and Queen, and consecrate themselves to her immaculate heart, to become members of her victorious cohort, or army, or the legion of Mary.

The 'Sun, Moon and Stars' are the mysterious things with which the Virgin Mary is beautifully decorated by God. And because they all give light, it implies that she is completely covered with light, that is to say, there is no stain of sin in her, neither original nor actual, as she was conceived and born immaculate.

In this great battle between the Virgin Mary and Satan the woman and the dragon, when Satan discovered that Mary is given a very important role to play in the economy of salvation by God, and also that she is the great and glorious Queen whom God had mandated to crush his head to pieces, and bring his glory to man, he dragged a third of the stars out of the sky using his tail, and threw them down to the earth *Rev. 12:4; Dan. 8:10*. These stars stand for those whom Satan has completely possessed *(including all the angels with whom he was thrown down from heaven)*. He uses them to fight the Virgin Mary, her children, the Catholic Church and her tradition. In obedience to their master *(the red dragon)*, these people infiltrate the church with the following un-Catholic practices, namely: *Modernism, Fundamentalism* and *Pentecostalism*. They are the brains behind the problems we have in the church today.

When the Virgin Mary was about to deliver into the world Jesus the Saviour, the dragon stood in front of her in order to eat up the child as soon as it was born. This was aimed at destroying the salvation of the human family. But suddenly the child was taken away, to the Throne of God in heaven *Rev. 12:4-5*. This is evident when Satan in the person of Herod, wanted to kill the infant Jesus, his mother took him away and protected his life in Egypt *Mt 2:13-15*. Also, after the death and burial of Christ, the dragon rejoiced and celebrated the victory not knowing that Jesus is the one that has won the victory. For he would later resurrect from the dead, ascend into heaven, to sit at the right hand of the Father *Mt. 28:5-7; Mk 16:19*. When the dragon eventually realized this, he found that he had lost the battle; so he became furious and began to pursue the woman clothed with the sun the Most Blessed Virgin, in order to destroy her. Unfortunately for him, the Virgin Mary who is full of grace, is always all - powerful and faithful to God. As he continued to pursue her, she was given the two wings of the great eagle to fly to her place of rest in the desert, away from the dragon's attack. In realizing this, the dragon poured out from his mouth a flood of water after her, in order to carry her away. At once, the earth came to her rescue. It opened and swallowed the flood *Rev. 12:6* and *13-16.*

Brethren, the '*Great Eagle*' whose wings were given to Mary stands for the '*Word*' of God especially the one in the Gospel according to St. John. The symbol of the Eagle is used because; the word soars above all the things of the earth, unafraid to the sun and speaks of the divine nature of Christ. The'*Two Wings*' of the eagle stand for faith and charity. That is, the word of God received by Mary, loved by her, and lived with grace, faith and charity.

The '*Desert*' to which the Virgin Mary fled for her rest, stands for heaven where she would be taken care of, made a Queen, glorified by God, Angels and Saints. The desert also stands for the hearts of the children of God, especially those who truly receive and welcome the Virgin Mary, love her, honour her, worship her, listen to her, obey her, consecrate themselves to her immaculate heart, and be abandoned completely to her service. It is in the hearts of these people, in union with the church, that she will be receiving her due honour, praise and glory in the world. It is the generation of these people *(the past, the present and the future)* that God had in mind when He decreed that all generation shall call Mary blessed *Ps. 45:17;Lk. 1:48.* No wonder, in her honour, the Church and her faithful children celebrate the following feasts, namely: *Immaculate Conception (Dec. 8), Birth of Mary (Sept. 8), Assumption (August 15), the Queenship of Mary (August 22nd),Presentation of Mary (Nov. 21), Immaculate Heart of Mary (Saturday following the 2nd Sunday after Pentecost), Our Lady of the Rosary (Oct. 7), Our Lady of Sorrows (Sept. 15),* as well as observing some special devotions to her, namely: *May Devotion, October Devotion, Saturday Devotions, the Recitation of the Holy Rosary, the Angelus and many others.*

The *'Flood of Water'* as vomited by the dragon stands for all attacks, blasphemies and abuses against the Virgin Mary. The flood also stands for all human agents of Satan within and outside the church, with their modern theological doctrines aimed at tarnishing the image of the Virgin Mary: to deny her privileges and honour, to restructure her devotion, to relegate her to the background, and to ridicule and discourage her faithful children and servants you and me. Whenever we hear people calling her an envelope, queen of the coast, and other blasphemous names, the truth is this: the dragon is once again vomiting that same flood of water *(of Rev. 12:15 the flood of blasphemy),* in order to destroy the Virgin Mary and her devotions so that she might be flushed out and forgotten completely. Thanks to God. The earth will always come to her rescue. It will continue to open and swallow up the flood as usual.

The *'Earth'* that opened and swallowed up the flood stands for all true devotions to Mary, made by the church and her children. With their internal and external devotions, they evangelize the world by preaching, singing, honouring, worshipping, serving, consoling, blessing and living the life of the Blessed Virgin everyday, thereby making her globally known, accepted, loved, followed, obeyed and glorified by all, from generation to generation. This is what we call the *"Swallowing of the flood of blasphemy"*. Whenever we glorify the holy name of Mary, we instantly become the earth, swallowing the flood of Satan.

Now, having lost the battle against Mary, Satan became increasingly furious with her and went off to fight the rest of her children, the brothers and sisters of Christ, you and me, whom the Bible declares as the people who truly obey the commandments of God and bear testimony to the gospel of Jesus Christ in *Rev. 12:17*. This goes to show that no one can truly obey the commandments of God and bear testimony to the gospel of Christ unless he is a child of Mary. This is what the Bible says and will remain true forever *Jn. 10:35*.

Children of God, by virtue of obedience to God and faith in Him, Mary has completely defeated the red dragon. She has crushed his head to pieces. The fact that God uses Mary to fight and destroy the dragon does not mean that Satan does not fear and respect Him, but that, since the dragon had destroyed His glory in man by means of a woman, Eve, it became necessary that He should also use a woman to pay him back in his own coin, so as to restore His glory in man. He had therefore, inspired and empowered his Blessed Mother right from the very moment of her personal existence, with so much hatred and skill, to uncover the malice and subtle snares of that wicked serpent such that he fears her more than he fears the angels and saints, and in a sense, more than God himself. It is not that God's power, anger and hatred are not perpetually greater than those of the Virgin Mary, but that, the dragon being very proud suffers perpetually more from being attacked and defeated by a humble handmaid of God. He feels severely marginalized and humbled by Mary's humility more than the power of God because what he has lost by pride, the Virgin Mary has gained by humility. This is how the promise and prophecy of God in *Gen. 3:15* is being fulfilled in *Rev. 12*. This is the total triumph of the Immaculate Heart of Mary the great woman of promise, prophecy, liberation and revelation. What a shame to you, Satan, and a very big shame to you all, human agents of Satan.

Finally, whoever has gotten the Virgin Mary has gotten everything that is precious in the very eyes of God. He has nothing to be afraid of because Satan will always be afraid of him in the same way as he is afraid of Mary. But he, who does not have Mary, has so many things to be afraid of because he moves in the emptiness of the grace of God. Satan will always find it easy to capture and tear such a person to pieces.

CHAPTER 9

THE POWERS OF THE MARIAN ROSARY OR THE HAIL MARY PRAYER

One day, I was in a public transport together with non
-Catholics. Somewhere along the road, we met some Catholics in rosary procession, carrying the statue of the Most Blessed Virgin Mary. At once those non-Catholics began to criticize them. They said that what annoyed them most was the Holy Rosary. So they asked, can the rosary save you people? Can the Virgin Mary save you? When I got up to answer these questions in order to defend my precious Catholic faith, someone interrupted me with this passage of the Bible, *"I am the way, the truth, and the life; no one comes to the Father except by me" Jn. 14:6.* He then said to me, why do you Catholics pray to Mary, since Jesus Christ is the only way to the Father? And why do you say the rosary? Is such practice in the Bible? Why not go straight-away to Jesus on your own and stop this idolatry? In answering these questions, I began first of all, by explaining to him *(and in a sense, to all non-Catholics)* that inasmuch as Jesus is the way to the Father, Mary is the one person who

leads everyone to Jesus, as we can see in *Jn. 2:5: "Whatever he tells you do it".* No one other than the Blessed Virgin, who conceived and bore Jesus into the world, can go straight-away to him. She alone is full of grace and worthy of the Saviour of the world. Jesus is God. He is gloriously unapproachable, and moves in unapproachable light**1 Tim. 6:16.** It is very clear that no one can go to the heavenly Father except by means of Jesus, but the question is this: How can we go to Jesus? By what means? We must first go to him, and from him and by him, to the Father. Only when we go by means of the heavenly Mother that we can actually get close to Jesus, and finally to the heavenly Father. She is the dwelling place of God. She is the one person to whom the Bible says: **"The Lord is inseparably with you".** The Blessed Virgin alone is the worthy means, the surest way, the straight and the immaculate way to go to Jesus. This truth is echoed by Christ Jesus in **Jn.19:27** when he said, **"Son, behold your mother",** that is to say, behold the Blessed Virgin, behold the way to Jesus. No wonder, in blessing the Saviour, Elizabeth was moved by the Holy Spirit and she began by blessing the Virgin Mary. She Blesses the Virgin Mary first, and Christ Jesus second: **"Blessed are thou among women, and blessed is the fruit of thy womb, Jesus" Lk.1:41-42.** It is not that the Blessed Virgin is more than Jesus or even equal to him, but that, in order to bless Jesus Christ more perfectly, we must begin by blessing the Virgin Mary. When we do this, we will no longer be the one blessing the Lord, but the Virgin Mary who alone is worthy of the Lord. This is what the Holy Spirit wishes to make known to the world through Elizabeth.

Now, since no one can go to the heavenly Father except by Jesus, and no one can go to Jesus except by Mary, it follows that no one can actually go to the heavenly Father except by means of the heavenly Mother.

In the Old Testament, when God planned to give His Law to the world on Mount Sinai, Moses was the instrument chosen by Him just as the Blessed Virgin (though in a more superior way) is the instrument chosen by Him, to bring into the world, Christ Jesus, who himself is the Divine Legislator. At that time, Moses was the instrument of communication between Heaven and earth, between Divinity and Humanity, and between God and the Jewish people.

Whenever God had a message for the chosen people and vice versa, He made use of Moses (the name Moses derives from both Egyptian 'mesu' and Hebrew origins 'moseh' meaning *"one drawn out"* and *"one who is born"*). At a point, some people became proud, and they became jealous of Moses; even as **Korah, Dathan and Abiram,** rejected him and rebelled against him with 250 Israelites who were leaders of the community. They hated Moses, they labeled him a deceiver; and instigated the people against him, and vowed never to listen to him anymore. They said to Moses: **"Moses, Moses, Moses, you have taken too much on yourself! Are you the only holy one in Israel? The whole** community, all its members, are consecrated, and God lives among them. Why have you set yourself higher than Yahweh's community? This God whom you claim to see everyday, who has been telling you all these, go and tell him that we do not want to listen to you anymore; we would want to come to see him as he is , and hear directly from his mouth. This is all we want".

So Moses went and told God what the people had said, and God told him not to worry; let them come, they will see me and they will surely hear from me. The Israelites opted to go straightaway to God on their own, as it is today with the Blessed Virgin and some people. Like the Israelites of old, they want to go straightaway to Jesus on their own, taking the Blessed Virgin to the background.

On that fateful day, when the Israelites got to Sinai, they stood at the foot of the mountain as demanded by God, and Moses climbed up the Mountain, to inform God of their presence. God, being an old ancient man, did something like this...*hmhmmmmm*...as if clearing His throat. At once the whole of Mountain Sinai was covered with heavy smoke and fire, like a blazing furnace. There was a heavy storm, there was thunder, and earthquake, rumblings and lightning; the earth opened and swallowed up many people Korah and his family and possession, Dathan and his family and possession, and Abiram and his family and possession, and all their followers. With a blazing fire, the Lord burnt up the 250 men, who had presented the incense, which was burnt disobediently on the altar. The number of people who died on that day was 14,700, not counting those who died in Korah's rebellion. In the end, the people who survived the anger of God ran straightaway to Moses and said, **"Is this what you have been encountering? Is this how this man speaks?** And Moses explained to them that God has not actually started speaking, as he was only clearing his throat, and getting ready to speak to them. In trembling and fear, they said to Moses: *"This man is only clearing his throat and all these things are happening. When he actually begins to speak, it means we will all die? Please, tell him not to speak to us any more. We have heard and seen enough. Go nearer to him and let him speak to you alone, we will listen to you. And whatever he tells you, we will do"* Ex.19:18-19; Ex. 20:18-21;Num.16:1-50;Deut.5:22-33.

My dear brethren, this is how it is going to be on the judgment day. The stone which the builders rejected as worthless must surely become the **corner stone.** The Blessed Virgin who is even more superior than Moses in the order of grace, must be honoured and glorified by all. Oh! The Immaculate Heart of Mary must surely triumph. All those who refuse to honour the Virgin Mary, to say the holy rosary, and to go to Jesus by means of Mary, both within and outside the church, whether good or bad; they will soon believe as our Father in heaven has promised. They will regret their stubbornness, they will regret their pride; and like the Israelites in the time of Moses, they will cry had I known. And they will forcibly honour the worthy Mother of

God all the more, even in hell fire, so as to make up for their unbelief. Now is the hour of grace. Repent and say your rosary before the Hammer strikes, before the anger of God strikes against you. It is the divine will of God that all men should have true devotion to the Marian Rosary.

At this juncture, let us analyze the holy rosary and see how much the points we will be making out of this analysis.

The term Rosary is taken from Latin origins that alternately imply a bed of roses, a garland of flowers, and a collection of nice quotations. It is a Catholic prayer devotion dedicated to the honour of the Virgin Mary, the *"Mystical Rose"* of God. The Most Holy Rosary of the Blessed Virgin is a priceless treasure through which we can learn to imitate the mysteries and virtues of the life, passion, death and glory of Jesus and Mary. It is a compendium of the entire gospel, that is to say, a concise and comprehensive account of the gospel. The rosary is a prayer in which the Holy Spirit invites us to contemplate the face of Christ through the eyes of his Mother Mary. Whenever a person thinks about the rosary, at the same time, he thinks about the redemptive history of man. The holy rosary is a gift of love from heaven. It was brought by Mary for the good of the human family. In saying the rosary, we walk hand in hand with Mary. The rosary is an arrangement of prayers, perfectly produced in heaven by the Most Blessed Trinity. It is aimed at bringing peace and salvation to the human family. It is composed of the following biblical prayers, namely:

a.   *Our Father, who art in heaven...*, by Jesus Christ who is the Second Person of the Blessed Trinity. This one is referred to as the Lord's Prayer *Mt. 6: 9-13; Lk. 11:2-4.*

b.   *Hail Mary, Full of Grace! The Lord is with Thee*, by God the Father who is the First Person of the Blessed Trinity. This one is offered to Mary through the Angel Gabriel, so is referred to as the Angelic Salutation *Lk. 1:28.*

c.   *Blessed art Thou among women, and Blessed is the fruit of Thy womb, Jesus*, by God the Holy Spirit who is the Third Person of the Blessed Trinity, through Elizabeth *Lk. 1: 41-42.*

The Holy Roman Catholic and Apostolic Church, received the most holy rosary from heaven, through **St. Dominic,** a Catholic priest, in the year **1214,** as a powerful means of converting the sinners. It all started when Dominic, seeing the state of damnation in which so many people were living their lives, especially the **Albigensians,** withdrew into a forest, near Toulouse, in France and prayed fervently for **3days** and **3nights,** appeasing the anger of God. He offered penances to God so much that his whole body became lacerated and he fell into a **coma.**

At this juncture the Blessed Virgin Mary appeared to him in company of three angels, and said: *"My beloved Dominic, do you know the weapon by which the Blessed Trinity wishes to use to reform the world?"* And Dominic answered, *"Oh, my lady, you know far better than I do because next to your son Jesus Christ, you have always been the chief instrument of our salvation".*

Then the Virgin Mary replied: *"I want you to know that in this kind of warfare, the battering ram has always been the Angelic Salutation (the Hail Mary) which is the foundation stone of the New Testament. Therefore, if you want to reach these hardened sinners and win them over to God preach my holy rosary"*.

Now having received the rosary directly from the immaculate hands of the heavenly Mother, Dominic became comforted, and burning with zeal for the conversion of sinners, he ran straightaway to the Cathedral. At once unseen angels rang the bells to gather the people together and Dominic began to preach.

At the very beginning of his sermon there was a heavy storm, and earthquake, the sun was darkened, and there was so much lightning and thunder, that everyone became very much afraid. The picture of the Virgin Mary exposed in a prominent place in the Cathedral began to raise her arms three times to heaven to call down the anger of God upon the people if they failed to get converted, to amend their lives, and seek the protection of the Mother of God. At the prayer of Dominic there was peace.

By means of these supernatural phenomena God wished to spread the new devotion of the holy rosary and to make it more widely known and acceptable by all people. In the end the people renounced their false beliefs, embraced the holy rosary and began to live Christian lives. This miraculous way in which the devotion to the holy rosary was established in the world is something of a parallel to the way in which the Eternal Father gave his Law to the world on Mount Sinai and obviously proves its value and importance.

With regards to the composition of the holy rosary, we could see that it is the prayers of the Most Holy Trinity.

Some people argue that although the rosary is in the Bible, its frequent repetition could be boring, annoying and unacceptable to God: for such could be likened to the prayers of pagans condemned by Jesus Christ Himself in *Mt. 6:7*. Therefore, it will not be good to say all the mysteries at a time, namely: the *Joyful*, the *Light*, the *Sorrowful*, and the *Glorious mysteries*.

Brethren, may I take you to *Mt. 26:39-44; Mk 14:35 39*. Here, we shall see Jesus Christ Himself saying one particular prayer repeatedly: *"Father, if this cup of suffering cannot be taken away from me unless I drink it, let your will be done."* So, if Jesus Christ Himself who is God could say one particular prayer repeatedly, what then is wrong in sinful creatures, saying the holy rosary repeatedly?

Again, if we go to *Rev. 4:8*, we shall see that the Angels always appear in the presence of God, before creation of the world, after creation, now that you are reading this book, and forever and ever, saying one particular prayer repeatedly: *"Holy, holy, holy, is the Lord God Almighty, who was, who is, and who is to come."* Assuming we suddenly find a Rev. Father on the street, walking and praying: *Holy, holy, holy,* people will say that he is mad, even his own parishioners, but he is not mad. For this is what the Angels are doing before God every moment.

Then, in the gospel of St. Luke, Jesus approves of a repetitious prayer made by the tax collector: a penitent sinner who strikes his chest in prayer to ask for God's mercy and pardon saying, through my own fault, through my own fault, through my most grievous fault *Lk. 18:13 14.*

Finally, in *Rm. 12:12,* the Bible asks us to pray without ceasing. No sincere prayer is in vain. Prayer is a dialogue with God. It is knowing happiness. Prayer is life. The more we pray the more closer we get to God. Prayer is power. A prayerful child of God is a powerful child of God.

Child of God, say your rosary without ceasing, in private and public places. Do not be discouraged by those who go about criticizing this devotion. They are the agents of Satan. Do not be ashamed. Say your rosary wherever you go, before the Blessed Sacrament, in the Chapel, in the Church, but not in the Holy Mass because the Mass is the greatest prayer that one can offer to God. Yet it was the Rosary that gave birth to the Holy Mass. For without the Hail Mary there will be no Mass. This is a mystery beyond human understanding. After the Mass comes the rosary. Also the Virgin Mary to whom the rosary is offered is there in the Mass, always at the foot of the altar, contemplating the sacrifice and immolation of her only son to the Eternal Father. We should be bold enough to say the rosary on the road, in market places, in various offices, on transit, at sports centers and so on and so forth. Remember that if we proclaim Jesus before all men, he will proclaim us before his father in heaven *Mt.10:32-33;Lk.12:8-9.* Do not be discouraged because some people might call you idol worshippers. Rather, be strengthened. If saying the rosary or praying the Hail Mary implies worshipping and adoring the Virgin Mary as they say, so be it; you are doing the will of God. It was He, who first of all worshipped and adored her, followed by the Angel Gabriel. If God and his angels could say the rosary, who are you, mortal man, not to say the rosary? Say your rosary in the same way as the goat chew the curd. Rosary is life. It is a mystical rose tree which comes straight from heaven and which is to be planted in the garden of our souls. It fills the devotee with grace necessary in life.

Some Catholics are in the habit of compromising the beautiful prayers of the holy rosary. They give up the rosary in order to accommodate public prayers made by protestant churches and their Pentecostal movements as though the rosary were inferior to the prayers of these people. This is wrong. This is a show of ignorance. You have the fullness of the truth and you give it up for a mode of worship that is not pleasing to God. Why not make them join in the rosary. This way grace of God could be given to them to come back to the truth which is only found in the Holy Roman Catholic and

Apostolic Church.

If I may ask, which man on God's own earth, whose prayers would be more agreeable, acceptable, and pleasing to the heart of God than those of the Virgin Mary whose heart is intimately united to the heart of God? Do you not know that your one 'Hail Mary' is more valuable, more powerful, and most efficacious than all the prayers that had ever been said or would ever be said by these protestant churches and their Pentecostal movements put together; the past, the present, and the future? It is so because the Hail Mary is the prayers of the Trinity. When you say the rosary, you pray with the Trinity. That is, you pray to God in union with God Himself. Tell me, is there anyone who can worthily pray to God than God Himself? The answer is emphatic NO! One with God is majority. Therefore whenever you begin to say the rosary, especially on transit and in other public places, do not give it up. Do not suspend it for any unCatholic prayers, no matter what anyone might say. This is a clear trick of Satan to deny you the graces you need at that point in time, through the Hail Mary. It is even wiser when in the midst of non-Catholics, especially the Pentecostals who are the present day magicians, a Catholic should hold on very tightly to the Marian Rosary because the angel of darkness is always itching to disguise into an angel of light.

When we honour the Blessed Virgin by the Hail Mary we bear witness to the Lord Jesus Christ that Mary is full of grace. In return, the Virgin Mary will honour us with heavenly graces in abundance.

By the Hail Mary God rejoices and glorifies Himself in the fact that in Mary, He has gotten back His true image and likeness which had been seized by Satan through the fall of man.

When we say the Hail Mary, we renew that same special joy and honour which was given to the Angel Gabriel when he was chosen among all the Angels to become God's Ambassador Extra-ordinary through whom this redemptive hymn of praise was sung for the first time since creation. Instantly he joins in the prayers and helps us present them to the Virgin Mary who will then present them worthily to the Trinity of Whom she is the Daughter, the Mother and the Spouse. How fortunate are you Christian soul to have the angel of salvation at your service!

One major reason why numerous sermons carried out today in the world fail to bear good fruits is because we try to cultivate on a piece of land which has not had any rain. When God planned to renew the face of the earth, He started by sending down rain from heaven. That rain was the angelic salutation the Hail Mary. It was through the Hail Mary that God discussed the New and Everlasting Covenant with Mary and Jesus was able to come to redeem the world. Jesus is that seed which God had planted in the world but this was through the Hail Mary. Therefore, the Hail Mary is the *"foundation stone"* of the New Testament. The Hail Mary or the Most Holy Rosary is richly empowered by God to offer solutions to all problems of the human family.

THE POWERS OF THE MARIAN ROSARY

In the Old Testament, when the Israelites became thirsty in the desert, Moses did not know what actually to do. Then, God called him and said: Moses, Moses, what do you have in your hand? And he replied it was the stick. God then asked him to strike it on the stone and as soon as he obeyed, at once water came out from the stone and the people drank to their satisfaction *Ex. 17:1-6*.

The stick of Moses symbolizes the Rosary of the Most Blessed Virgin Mary in the New Testament. The stone upon which he struck out water symbolizes Jesus Christ the Rock of Ages. That same rock which the builders rejected as worthless, but is now the Cornerstone *1 Pt. 2:6 8; Eph. 2:20; 1 Cor. 10:4*. The desert and those Israelites stand for souls in search of lost grace *Rm. 3:23*. If we strike our rosary upon Jesus the Rock, that is to say, if we pray to God by means of the rosary of the Virgin Mary, the water we shall drink shall be better than that of the Israelites of Old. It will be that same water given by Jesus Christ to the Samaritan woman the life giving water life everlasting in heaven *Jn. 4:13-15*.

My brother, my sister, that thing you have in your hand, I mean the rosary of the Blessed Virgin, is the solution to all your problems, yet you have continued to move about from one church to another. The truth is that you have not said your rosary enough. Today, God is asking you the same question he asked Moses his servant: my child, what do you have in your hand? Is that not the rosary of my Blessed Mother? Why not strike it on the stone (Jesus Christ) so that your problems will be solved.

The Hail Mary is an irresistible prayer before the throne of the Divine Trinity. It shakes the whole of heaven and moves the Almighty God about on His throne, leaving Him without a choice and He bends down to listen to you. What a great weapon to bring down God from heaven; to bring Him down from His throne! Is this not wonderful?

The Hail Mary is a *Blessed Dew* that falls down from heaven upon the souls of the predestinate. It gives them a marvelous spiritual fertility so that they can grow in all virtues. The more the garden of a soul is watered by the Hail Mary, the more enlightened that person's intellect will become, the more zealous his heart and the stronger his weapons against the enemy.

The Hail Mary is a *sharp* and *flaming sword* which when joined to the word of God, will give the preacher the strength to pierce and convert the most hardened hearts. The Rosary is the *water* for washing the sinner and reclaiming those who have strayed away. It is the *rope* that brings people to the knowledge of Jesus and Mary. It lessens our sufferings and bad conditions. It provides blessings for child delivery, peace and love. The Rosary is a reliable *weapon* that batters the head of Satan. It is that *chain* with which we can chain Satan forever *Rev. 20:1-3.* It is the *bullet* that gives us victory over our bad situation. The Rosary is a necessary *weapon* which transforms every bad situation to a good one. It is the *progress* of the righteous, the *deliverance* of the captives, and the *power* of the powerless. It strengthens and reawakens the lukewarm. It is the *deliverance* of the sick, especially those who have little or no hope to live again.

The family that says the rosary together stays together. They will enjoy peace, harmony, love, progress and divine protection. Therefore every community, every nation, every race on God's own earth: black or white, rulers and their subjects, the rich and the poor, in fact the whole world: Christians and non-Christians, Israelites and Gentiles, Catholics and non-Catholics, should come together as one people to say the Hail Mary. The Bible says that, whenever two or more people come together to pray, God Himself will be in their midst *Mt. 18:20.* If this is the case, then how more active and mighty will become His divine presence in the midst of the people that come together, not just to pray but also to acknowledge and honour God's own words which is the Hail Mary.

Children of God, though individual prayers are greatly important and very enriching, you should always come together in groups and offer your rosary to God. The benefit of group prayers is far better than the benefit which is obtainable in individual prayers. When one person says the Hail Mary, the blessings given to him are multiplied by one. But when people come together to say the Hail Mary as a group, each person's benefit would be the quantities of Hail Mary recited multiplied by the number of the individuals in that group. Let no one isolate himself.

The individual devotion of isolated souls is often a spark in the middle of darkness without the influence of a flame. The Hail Mary is a spiritual remedy. Through our union of charity in praying the Holy Rosary we inject this spiritual remedy into the souls of others as **spiritual medicine.** In this way, those who are strong uphold the weak: those who are fervent inspire the lukewarm: those who are spiritually rich enrich the poor. Union with others will do more than inflame the zeal of all of us: it will make it commonly strong: the strong Army of Mary.

If we work with one another we will be ten times as strong. And, if we form a closely united battalion matching under Our Lady's banner we will become invisible.

My dear brethren, do you want peace to reign in your various families, communities and countries? Are you seeking for your country's independence? Do you want her freedom? Do you want to quench all these bombings and terrorist attacks? Do you truly want peace to reign supreme in this deeply troubled world? If you do then let us come together and launch a Rosary Crusade for peace in the world. This way peace can be concealed to the whole world through the Blessed Virgin, the Queen of Peace. Think of the power of a river. It is made up of tiny drops of water, numberless tiny drops of rain. Together these tiny drops make a mighty river, which can carry heavy ships and change arid deserts into fertile farms and gardens. So, too, the Rosary Crusade, the rosaries of countless persons all over the world become an immense and irresistible spiritual force for peace.

It is of great importance that at the end of the prayers of the Holy Rosary we should offer the following prayers for the Holy Father (the Pope): one Our Father, one Hail Mary, and one Gloria. Many Catholics do not know this.

The Rosary is the *good name* for all Christians and all those who keep the commandments of God. It is the *consoler* of the sorrowful and the *elevator* of the fallen. It is a *quiet fighter* in a visible warfare. It is that *catapult* with which king David battered the head of Goliath. In *I Sam. 17:48 51*, David defeated and killed Goliath with a catapult and a stone. While the *catapult* symbolizes the rosary of the Virgin Mary, the *stone* he slung at Goliath stands for Jesus Christ the Rock of ages. We can see these mysterious stones around the rosary in the form of beads.

The rosary is the weapon that moves all creatures to worship and adore God. According to the letter of Saint Paul to the Philipians, "Whenever the name of Jesus is mentioned, in honour of this holy name all beings in heaven, on earth, and beneath the earth fall on their knees, and openly proclaim that Jesus Christ is Lord" *Philipians 2:10-11*. If this is the case then the Hail Mary is the greatest weapon to make all creatures adhere to this. Think how many times do we mention this name as we recite the Hail Mary in the full rosary. That is the number of times we make all creatures to submit to the holy name of Jesus. While some worship this name rejoicing and smiling (Angels and Saints in heaven and holy souls on earth), others worship this same name weeping and gnashing their teeth (Lucifer, his fallen angels, souls in hell and human agents of Satan on earth).

Child of God, why not pick up your rosary against the enemy. The more you say the rosary, the more you make him bow to the holy name of Jesus, and the more he is kept far away from you. For each time he gets up to reach at you, the more he forcibly bows down to the holy name of Jesus as many times as mentioned in your Hail Mary. And thus will have no time for himself, let alone attack you.

The Hail Mary is the weapon that makes disobedient Satan to become obedient. It is the great cane that flogs him to submission.

The Hail Mary destroys occultism. Who is that evil man, that cultic man disturbing your peace? Pick up your rosary and the enemy will flee.

The Rosary is everything good. It is the *weapon* used by the Angel Gabriel when he carried the message of Annunciation to Mary. It is the *king* of all weapons of warfare. With the Marian Rosary, the Egyptians you see today, you will see no more. It is the weapon that goes to chaotic situation the weapon that goes to war and war ends instantly the weapon that goes to a place of iniquity and brings about repentance the weapon that binds Satan and causes him headache. It is the *strength* of the Holy Roman Catholic and Apostolic Church. Anyone who uses the rosary is knowledgeable, anyone who throws it away, throws away all the good that should come to him. The rosary is not for the proud or those who castigate it or the Virgin Mary. It is for the humble because it is a humble prayer of petition. It implies the recognition of a want or insufficiency and an appeal for God's help. It is *persistent prayer,* that is, a prayer without ceasing. In the Gospel, Jesus Christ acknowledges and praises the poor and the humble who press their petitions until they are heard: like the widow in the parable of the corrupt judge in *Lk. 18:1-8* or the Canaanite woman. This woman came to Jesus and pleaded to Him to deliver her daughter of a demon that had terribly tormented her. And Jesus replied, *"I have been sent only to those lost sheep; the people of Israel"*. And as if this was not enough, again He said to her, *"it is not right to take the food meant for children and throw it to dogs"*.

Children of God, if you were to be the Canaanite woman,

would you continue to petition Jesus over your problem? Would you continue patiently to petition your better, husband, parish priest, boss, neighbour and what have you? Of course no. You would abandon Jesus altogether. Some may even say to him, 'to hell with your gift'. This is how many people pray to God today. People are impatient. There is no humility. In the end, they go home empty handed; blaming and cursing God, and moving about from one church to another, looking for instant miracles and losing their souls to the enemy. It takes a lot of humility and patience to get our petitions granted by God. The Canaanite woman persisted in humility, patience, contemplation and faithfulness. At last, Jesus granted her request-Mt. 15:21-28. Let everyone emulate her. For this is the lesson of this gospel passage.

When repetition is the sign of deep distress together with a confidence that will not be disappointed, it is a sign of authentic prayer.

The rosary is not the type of prayer people rush and go. It is a *contemplative prayer*, a meditation on the mysteries of the Lord's life as seen through the eyes of his mother Mary who was closest to him. To pray the rosary is to contemplate with Mary the Lord made flesh, crucified and raised for our salvation. The rosary is symbolized by that *number of fish* purposely counted by Jesus and his disciples in *Jn. 21:10 11*. The number was a *hundred and fifty three* in all, signifying the *one hundred and fifty three* **(153)** Hail Marys. That is to say, **150** Hail Marys in the original fifteen **(15)** decades plus the first three Hail Marys on the rosary, making it **153** Hail Marys in all before the recent addition of the Light Mysteries by the Holy Father, Pope John Paul II. Jesus so counted the fish so as to emphasize on the importance of the holy rosary and the need for us to say full rosary without ceasing.

The Rosary has *missionary power*. It combines petition with contemplation of the mysteries of Christ. A prayer of this kind is an education in the Faith and one of the surest and most effective ways to conversion, which is totally the result of prayer.

The Holy Church of Christ has made available a lot of indulgences to her faithful children who recite the holy rosary. Indulgences are partial or total remissions of punishments due for sins that already have been forgiven. The word 'Indulgence' is taken from Latin 'Indulgentia' and Middle English roots referring to *"yielding to the wishes of"* another and *"gentleness"*. The church can grant indulgences to individuals because of the super-abundance of merits gained for humanity by Jesus Christ and because of the great spiritual bounty available to humankind through the cumulative Christian prayer, works, and witness of the entire communion of saints.

There are two kinds of indulgences, namely: *partial* and *plenary* indulgences. Partial indulgences are those indulgences, through which part of one's temporal punishment for sin is remitted. Plenary indulgences are those indulgences, through which all of one's temporal punishment for sin is wiped away for ever.

The practice of granting indulgences dated back to the early Church, but got much emphasis from the Holy Father, **Pope Urban II** during the 11th century, the time of the great crusades. By the 13th century this practice became formerly accepted by the Church. In 1343 **Pope Clement VI** incorporated the concept of indulgences into Church Law. In 1476 **Pope Sixtus IV** declared that the spiritual merits gained by individuals on earth and in heaven can assist those in purgatory. From that time Church leaders began to dispense various kinds of indulgences from an official *thesaurus*, that is, a Church *"treasury"*, of graces and merits.

In saying the rosary, there is a plenary indulgence at the hour of death. For each groups of five mysteries recited a person gains 10years and 10 quarantines. Those who take part in or attend the Rosary Procession receive 7years and 7quarantines. Those who openly wear the rosary out of devotion and to set a good example for others receive 100days of indulgence. Just a kiss of love on the rosary gives you 500days of plenary indulgence. That is to say, if you were to spend 500days in purgatory, it will now be 500-500 and that is zero. That is to say, your days in purgatory are over. You can now jump into heaven.

Christian soul, I ask you, what are you still waiting for? Pick up your rosary. Immerse yourself in it. Wear it around your neck. Give it a kiss of love. Oh! Recite it without ceasing. This is an open secret of heaven. Today, it has been given to you. Be wise and make the best out of this wonderful privilege given to you. I tell you, you shall become hilarious on the last day.

The Rosary *highlights Mary's* maternal role. It acquaints us with the spiritual motherhood of Mary and especially as regards her motherly role of *educatrix* in prayer. It teaches us to talk with Mary as we talk with our mother, opening our heart to her humility and love and so acquiring the attitude of soul fundamental for the kingdom of God. No one can please the Virgin Mary more than by saying the salutation which the Most Adorable Trinity sent to her, and by which she was raised to the dignity of Mother of God.

By the word **Ave** which is the name **Eve,** God preserved her from all sin and its attendant misery which the first woman had been subject to.

The name **Mary** which means **lady of light** shows that God has filled Mary with wisdom and light, like a shining star to light up heaven and earth.

The words **Full of Grace** show that the Holy Spirit has showered upon the Virgin Mary the fullness of His divine grace; that she is able to give these graces in abundance to those who ask for them through her as **Mediatrix.**

When we say the **Lord is with thee** we renew the indescribable joy that was Mary's own, when the **Eternal Word** became incarnate in her womb.

And at the words **Blessed is the fruit of thy womb, Jesus,** the whole of heaven rejoices with Mary to see Jesus Christ her son adored and glorified for having saved mankind.

Thus, the more we honour and bless the Virgin Mary, the more we honour and bless Jesus Christ, because we honour and bless the Blessed Virgin only that we may honour and bless Jesus Christ the more perfectly, since we go to her only as the way by which we are to find the end we are seeking which is Jesus Christ. We get close to Jesus and ultimately to the Father.

Until recently, outside the mysteries of the **15 decades**, that is, minus the first **3 Hail Marys,** the Rosary has the same number of Angelic Salutations as there are psalms in the book of the Psalms of David. Therefore, while the book of the Psalms is referred to as the **Psalter** of David, the Rosary is referred to as the **Psalter** of Jesus and Mary. In the early Church simple and uneducated people were not able to say the Psalms, so the Rosary was held to be just as fruitful for them as the Psalms of David were to others. But the Rosary is more valuable than the Psalms for three reasons:
1. While the Angelic Salutation bears the nobler fruit

which is the Word Incarnate in Mary, Jesus Christ, the Psalms only prophesy His coming.
2. Just as the real thing is more important than its prefiguration, so is the Hail Mary more important than   the Psalms.
3. While the Hail Mary is the direct work of the Trinity, the Psalms were made through human instrument.

The Rosary is that *New Hymn* which King David prophesied about in *Ps. 144:9.* It was prophesied as a New Hymn because it was to be sung in the New Testament. The Old Hymn was the one which the Israelites of Old sang to thank God for creating them, choosing them, blessing them; and saving them from the hands of their enemies, the Egyptians *Ex. 15: 1-18.* The New Hymn which is the Hail Mary is the one which we *(the Christians)* shall sing as the New Israelites, to thank God, for saving us from the hands of our greatest enemy, Lucifer himself. Therefore, the Hail Mary is a *Hymn of praise* and *thanksgiving* to God for restoring the fallen human race to life. So, those who refuse to honour Mary or say the Hail Mary, also refuse to appreciate the work of God. Such persons are ungrateful. To them Jesus says, *"There were ten men who were healed; where are the other nine? Why is it that only one person came to thank God?" Lk. 17: 17-18.* That is to say, why is it that after God has healed the wounds of this fallen humanity by means of the Hail Mary and restored it to life, some people still refuse to thank Him by refusing to say the Hail Mary. The greatest event in the whole history of the world was the *Incarnation* of the *Eternal Word* by whom the world was redeemed and peace was restored between God and man. Our Blessed Virgin was the Instrument chosen by God for this tremendous event, and it was put into effect when she was greeted with the Angelic Salutation the Hail Mary. It is a new hymn of the law of grace and the joy of angels and men.

By the Hail Mary the Virgin Mary became blessed among women, Angel Gabriel became blessed among all the angels, God became man, a Virgin became the mother of God, the souls of the just were delivered from Limbo, the empty thrones in heaven were filled, sin was forgiven, grace was given to man, the sick became well, the dead came back to life, the exiles came back home, the anger of God was appeased, and men obtained eternal life. O, the Hail Mary is a *sign* of the mercy and grace of God to mankind. It is a *Rainbow* in heaven. And according to Blessed Alan, *"Those who recite the rosary everyday have a very great assurance of salvation."*

Finally, the Hail Mary *(or the Marian Rosary)* is that bridge of Salvation by which we might pass with safety over the stormy sea of this present world, and reach the happy heaven of paradise. That is to say, it is a means of finding solution to all our problems, both spiritual and physical. No wonder, before a man is created, God has given him a rosary. In each mystery five decades, in each decade ten Hail Marys. These correspond to the number of fingers God has given to every man. Therefore, child of God, you have been given a rosary *(i.e. your fingers)* before you were created. So, never you relent in saying your rosary everyday.

C H A P T E R   1 0

MARY
THE THRONE OF GRACE
OR FULL OF GRACE

When a person entrusts himself to the Most Gracious Virgin Mary with a childlike confidence, he or she will be filled with divine grace because the Virgin Mary Herself is the *"Throne of Divine Grace."* In the letter of St. Paul to the Hebrews, the Blessed Virgin is described as the throne of grace. In this biblical passage, St. Paul advises us to always go to Mary whenever we fall short of grace. He maintains that if we confidently go to her, we shall obtain God's mercy and grace in abundance. In his own words, he says, *"Let us be brave, then, and approach God's throne, where there is grace. There we will receive mercy and find grace to help us just when we need it"* Heb. 4:16.

In the same way as God the Father made an assemblage of all the waters and named it sea, He also made an assemblage of all his graces and named it Mary. This is evident in the message of the Angel Gabriel to the Virgin Mary. At the annunciation, the Angel Gabriel addressed Mary as *"Full of grace" Lk 1:28.* Here the angel did not call the holy Virgin by her proper earthly name: *Miryam* or *Mary,* but by this new name: *'full of grace.'* The angel thus greeted the Blessed Virgin as the person whose name is *'full of grace,'* that is, if we equate Mary with *'full of grace'* or Mary equals to *'full of grace.'* In other words, Mary means Grace of God. By the word *'Full'* it implies that something or somebody is completely filled. So for Mary to be full of grace implies that she is completely and supper-abundantly filled with God's graces such that she distributes them to whom she wills, as much as she wills, as she wills, and when she wills. In this way, she is confirmed as *'Mediatrix of all graces.'* In all truth, Mary is full of grace. This manner of address is unique in the Bible and is reserved exclusively for her. Because of its importance with regard to her, *Pope John Paul II* made the following detailed analysis of it in his Encyclical: *Redemptoris Mater* **or** *The Mother of the Redeemer:*

a. God the Father of Our Lord Jesus Christ has blessed us in Christ with every spiritual blessing *Eph. 1:3.* His Divine Plan, which was fully revealed to us with the coming of Christ, is eternal and eternally linked to Christ. It includes everyone, but it reserves a special place for the *"Woman"* who is the Mother of Him to Whom the Father has entrusted the work of salvation.

b. As the Second Vatican Council says, "She is already prophetically foreshadowed in that promise made to our first parents after their fall into sin *Gen. 3:15.* Likewise she is the Virgin who is to conceive and bear a Son, Whose name will be called Emmanuel" *Is 7:14.*

c.   Mary is *"full of grace"* because of that blessing with which the Father has filled us *"in the heavenly places with Christ."* It is a spiritual blessing that is meant for all people and that bears in itself fullness and universality. It flows from the love that, in the Holy Spirit, unites the consubstantial Son to the Father. At the same time, it is a blessing poured out through Jesus Christ upon human history until the end: upon all people.

d.   This blessing, however, refers to Mary in a special and exceptional degree: for she was greeted by Elizabeth as *"blessed among women" Lk. 1:42.* In the soul of this Daughter of Zion, there is manifested, in a sense, all the glory of grace, the grace that the Father has given us in His beloved Son.

e.   In the language of the Bible, grace means a special gift, which according to the New Testament has its source precisely in the Trinitarian life of God Himself, God who is love *1 Jn. 4:8.* The fruit of this love is the *"election"* spoken of in *Eph. 1: 4- 6.* On the part of God, this election is the eternal desire to save humankind through a sharing in His own life - *2 Pt 1:4:* it is a salvation through a sharing in supernatural life.

Children of God, taking into consideration the account of the

Holy Father, we could see that Mary's privileged and grace-filled origin is the Father's final step in preparing humanity to receive its Redeemer in human form. Mary's fullness of grace exists in three different degrees according to Theologians. Firstly, there is the absolute fullness of grace that exists in Christ Jesus. Taking into consideration only God's ordinary power, there can be no greater grace than this. It is the inexhaustible source of all the grace that human beings receive from the *Fall* till the end of time. It is also the source of the beatitude of the just, for Jesus Christ has merited all the effects of our predestination. Secondly, there is the fullness of superabundance that is Mary's special privilege. It is named thus, because it is like a *spiritual river* that has poured out its abundance upon the souls of human beings throughout the ages. Thirdly, there is the fullness of sufficiency common to all the just and which made them capable of performing those meritorious acts that lead them to eternal life.

The Theologians further explained that Mary's fullness of grace did not cease to increase up to the time of her death. Hence, they speak of **(a)** *Her initial fullness or plenitude;* **(b)** *her second sanctification at the moment of Jesus' conception; and* **(c)** *her final fullness at the instant of her entry into glory.*

Now, having gone through all these facts, rooted in the Bible and clarified by the church, I say with St. Paul: Let us be brave, then, and run quickly to Mary Full of grace that we may receive God's mercy and grace in abundance. The Bible says that no one can please God without his grace *Rm. 3:24; Rm. 11:5-6; Eph. 2:8-9; Titus 2:12*, and since all men have sinned and fallen short of God's grace *Rm. 3:23*, whereas Mary herself is full of grace, everyone should co-operate with her. In *Ps. 45:9*, she stands clearly on the right of God's throne so that in her fullness of grace, she may intercede to obtain God's mercy and grace for those who seek her intercession.

Beloved brothers and sisters come and let us quickly run to Mary the *"Throne of grace"*. She alone is the *"Treasurer"* and *"Dispenser"* or *"Distributrix"* of God's divine grace. Have confidence. She is good and generous. Does a mother ever refuse her child anything she can give to him? Of course not. In giving to you, she continues to give to Jesus because she knows that he lives in you and that whatever is done to the least of his brothers is done to him *Mt. 25:40*. She desires to give you more than you desire to receive because she loves you more and loves Jesus in you more than you can ever love yourself. And she knows what is good for you more than you know. Your sinfulness is great indeed yet it will never be greater than Mary's motherly love for you. She favors you not because you are good but because she is good. Does she cease to be good because you are bad? Of course no. She is goodness itself. All you need to do is to ensure that your intentions are in conformity with her intentions because her intentions are always in conformity with the designs of God, and they are always realized *Lk. 1:38; Jn. 2:5; Lk. 2:51; Jn. 2:7-10*. Therefore, each time you desire something, ask Mary your Mother to make her intentions in the matter come true and be rest assured that you will get either what you desire or something better. This is evident at the wedding feast of Cana, in Galilee. The Most Gracious Virgin, by her prayers and intercessions, provided the couple with a wine far better than the one they previously desired.

Now let us go to the Gospel of St. John, to analyze in details, the events that took place in Cana. What role did Our Blessed Virgin play at the wedding? What is the significance of the event with regard to our relationship with God and Mary? The answer is in the next page.

C H A P T E R 1 1

MARY
THE ROLE OF MARY AT THE WEDDING OF CANA
JOHN 2

After his return to Galilee, Jesus and Mary were invited to Cana to attend the wedding of a young couple whom they knew. The Bride came from Bethlehem and was related to St. Joseph's family. The Groom came from Capharnaum and was related to St. Anne.

Jesus considered this wedding of great importance for several reasons. He wished to begin his public ministry by sanctifying and blessing the institution of marriage. He wanted to strengthen and to unite his new disciples by performing his first public miracle among them. He wished to refute the unjust criticism which had arisen against him during his prolonged absence from home, to the effect that he was neglecting his work, his mother and his relatives. Above all, he wished to reveal to the world how much we need the intercession of his mother Mary.

According to history and divine revelations, on the second day after his arrival, in the evening, Jesus preached in the temple before all the guests. He spoke of pleasures which are permissible, of the motives with which one might indulge in them, of their limitations, and of the caution and restraints that must accompany them. Then he spoke of marriage, of the mutual obligations of husband and wife, of continence and chastity, and also of spiritual marriage. He also gave the young couple some private instructions.

The next morning, at nine O'clock, the wedding ceremony took place. Before the banquet, Jesus organized a remarkable game for the men in the garden. He placed various flowers, plants and fruits around a large table on which there was a pointer that rotated on a pivot until it stopped before the prize of the person who had twirled it. In this game, nothing occurred by mere chance. Each prize somehow had a definite significance related to the qualities and faults of its winner. When a player won his particular prize, Jesus made a brief and profound comment. Yet the personal application of his word was grasped only by the man to whom they were directed. The others found in them merely some broadly edifying teaching. But the individual himself was deeply moved and felt that Jesus had indeed seen into the most secret thoughts of his heart and conscience.

When the bridegroom won a very striking exotic fruit, Jesus spoke about marriage, chastity, and purity. And when Jesus handed him his prize, the young man was stirred to the depths of his soul. He turned pale, and underwent a mystical purification in which he was supernaturally liberated from the unclean lusts of the flesh. At the same time the bride, who was sitting among the women at some distance, had a fainting spell and experienced something similar, while the Virgin Mary held her in her arms and helped her to revive. All these happened without anyone noticing them. Thereafter the young couple seemed definitely brighter and purer in appearance. The other disciples, after they had eaten the fruit which they won, became strengthened to conquer their passions, and to resist future temptations. When the game was over, everyone returned to the festival hall.

There was a lamb which had been roasted for the wedding feast. When the bridegroom brought the carving knife to Jesus, the Lord reminded him of his prediction at the banquet when they were boys, after the Finding in the Temple, that he would attend his wedding. The young husband now became very thoughtful as he recalled what Jesus had said then. He had completely forgotten this incident of his childhood.

While carving the lamb, Jesus gave an instructive talk to the guests. He spoke of the lamb being separated from the flock and led to be killed. Then he explained how, in the process of roasting, the flesh was purified by fire. He said the carving up of the parts, symbolized the way in which the followers of the Lamb of God must leave those to whom they are attached by bonds of flesh and blood. And while distributing the pieces of meat to the guests, he said that just as the lamb had been taken from its companions and had been put to death in order to provide food for many persons, so too he who wished to follow the Lamb of God must leave his home and neighbourhood and family, and put his passions to death, for then he could become a source of spiritual food by which he could unite his fellow men with one another and with the Heavenly Father, through the Lamb of God.

When the wine suddenly got finished, Mary moved straight away to Jesus and said, *"Son, they have no wine left."* Although nobody told Mary about this, she was able to know because she is full of grace and possesses the power and wisdom of God - *Wisdom 7:25.* Then Jesus got up and said to her, *"Woman, what do you want from me? Do you not know that my hour has not yet come?* Apart from maintaining the word *"woman"* by which the Bible *(and the prophets)* describe Mary from Genesis to Revelation in order to make her known to the people at the occasion *(and in a sense, to all men),* as the woman with whom he would restore God's glory to man, he also wanted to favour her humility.

The question *"do you not know that my time has not yet come?"* implies that Mary did know but she humbly did not say any other thing to Jesus rather she said to the servants, *"Whatever he (Jesus) tells you do it".* Then having done her part as intercessor for others, she humbly returned to her place among the women, knowing that her son who always was indeed the promised Messiah. At the same time they had become better men and women, more devout and more united.

The surprise comment of the chairman of the occasion concerning the new wine which was of better quality than the old shows that, the world gives the strong wine first and then the poorer, but in the kingdom of God it is not so. Pure water was changed into excellent wine, to demonstrate that negligence and lukewarmness should give way to love and zeal; that the water of lukewarmness should be changed into the wine of love and enthusiasm, as demonstrated by the Lord Himself when he changed bread and wine into his Body and Blood in order that he would remain with us until the end, to strengthen and console us.

The words *"Best Wine"* symbolize the quality and efficacy of the prayers and intercessions of the Virgin Mary. That is to say, her prayers and requests are the best before God. This implies that if we unite our prayers and petitions with those of Mary, they would turn out to become the best and the most acceptable before God.

Again, after Jesus had said his time had not yet come, he went ahead and granted the request of Mary. The lesson here is that, child of God, may be the time has not yet come for God to grant your requests, for Him to give solution to that problem which has made you look as tiny as a stick of broom, obeys her according to *Lk. 2: 51*, would obey her. Mary knows her son and her son knows her. Both of them work hand in hand. So, Jesus told the servants to fill the six jars with water. He then asked them to take some to the chairman of the occasion. Children of God, if I were the servants, I would have said to Jesus, *"Master, the Chairman has not requested for water."* Yes, because I knew it was water that was in those jars but Jesus knew it had turned into wine. This is the *"manifestation"* of Jesus Christ at the request of Mary. This is Christ's first miracle of nature. It shows the Blessed Virgin as the *Miracle of the miracles of nature* and also as a *woman full of generosity*. There was no way Jesus would have disobeyed his mother, for he was the one who gave the commandment: *"Obey your father and your mother"* and so, cannot contradict himself *Ex. 20:12; Deut. 5:16; Sirach 3:3-4; Eph. 6:2.*

After the chairman had tasted the wine, he said to the Bridegroom, *"Is anything wrong with you? Everyone first serves the best wine, and when they have drunk freely, then that which is poorer in quality. But you have kept the best wine until now? As if to say, perhaps you wanted to drink it only with your kinsmen?*

By this incomprehensible miracle, everyone was filled with awe and wonder, including the relatives of Jesus. They were utterly changed in their attitude toward the Lord. They now suddenly became convinced of his power, dignity, and divine mission. Henceforth they believed with firm faith that he that problem which has made you a laughing stock in the society, an object of caricature; that problem which has made you look for help in places of divine absence. It seems to you this problem will never be over as almost everyone now makes mockery of you. It seems that time is running against you. You have been rejected, dejected, deserted, isolated and abandoned by all, both friends and family members. It seems to you there is no more hope. You have booked Masses upon Masses: you have fasted for so long: you have done one Novena prayer or the other yet nothing seems to be working out for you. Oh, you have no more wine!

Child of God, now let me ask you, what will you do? Will you relent? Will you give up your hope? Or will you begin to curse and attack God as some faithless Catholics do this day? Here is the secret: the solution to your problem is this, by Mary's intervention God will provide you with a new wine. And the best one at that. That is to say, He will hasten to grant your petition even earlier than the time He had previously decided. Jesus has used this miracle to teach that only the Blessed Virgin Mary can worthily make God to do something even when his time to do so has not come. For inasmuch as Jesus is all powerful by nature, Mary is all powerful by grace. She alone can change the plan of God. But there are certain conditions that we must meet before we can enjoy this privilege.

1.*We must first of all invite the Blessed Virgin Mary into our life then God will come in. This is evident in Jn. 2:1-2. The couple at the wedding feast, invited Mary   first, and Jesus second, and they were rewarded with the best wine.*

2. We must be ready to listen to Mary at all times and   p u t her advice into practice, just as the servants did in verse five. Whenever we do this, we shall drink the best wine in return.

The greatest lesson of the miracle of Cana is that Jesus wanted to reveal to us how much we need the *"intercession"* of the Most Holy Mary. The same way she saved the bridegroom from public embarrassment, which could have resulted from the shortage of wine, she will save those who seek her intercession from the embarrassment of being damned eternally due to the shortage of divine grace.

After the banquet the young couple felt themselves dead to all carnal desires, and consented to live in continence with one another for three years, as a way of sacrifice to the Heavenly Father. And Jesus blessed them.

Finally, in *verse eleven*, Jesus gives more glory to his Father in heaven by submitting himself to his Blessed Mother. O, how perfectly we glorify God when to please Him, we submit ourselves to the Most Glorious Virgin Mary after the example

of Jesus Christ who is our *sole exemplar.*

THE INSEPARABILITY OF
JESUS AND MARY

In an entirely special and exceptional way, Mary is united with Jesus Christ. It is precisely in her that the Incarnation of the Word, the *hypostatic union* of the Son of God with human nature, is accomplished and fulfilled. In her is manifested the *"glory of grace"* that God the Father has bestowed upon us in His beloved Son *Eph. 1:6-7*. She has been redeemed in a more sublime manner. By virtue of the richness of the grace of the beloved Son, by reason of the *redemptive merits* of Him who willed to become her Son, Mary was preserved from the inheritance of original sin. In this way, from the first moment of her conception, that is, of her existence, she belonged to Christ, sharing in salvific and sanctifying grace and in that love that has its beginning in the beloved Son of the Eternal Father, who through the Incarnation became her own Son. Consequently, through the power of the Holy Spirit, in the order of grace, which is a participation in the Divine Nature, the Blessed Virgin receives life from Him to Whom she herself gave life as a Mother.

In all truth, Jesus and Mary are inseparable. They are that single way of life which we aspire to reach and share. God has in so many mysterious ways apart from the one we have just discussed, made manifest the *inseparability* of Jesus and Mary. In the book of Ezekiel, chapter forty- seven, verses one to nine *(Ezk 47: 1-9)*, there are two streams from the temple's gate, flowing towards one direction to the east, which is the direction of God and that is heaven. These two streams represent graces from Jesus and Mary.

This implies unity or oneness: that the grace from Jesus and the one from his mother Mary are all the same, for the glory of God. Both graces are meant for our salvation, that is, while the grace from the Virgin Mary protects, the one from Jesus saves. Thus, man's salvation is dependent on the combination of Jesus and Mary since the two are graciously inseparable. To win the battle against the enemy, to find solution to our problems, we must embrace these two pillars *Jesus* and *Mary*. Imagine Samson the great warrior, although Jesus and Mary were not yet born at the time, he sought salvation and power from God by embracing them. By means of these mysterious pillars, he was able to conquer his enemies the Philistines *Judges 16:28-30*. These are the two pillars which when faithfully embraced by children of God, will lead them to heaven. These are the two pillars of the church, with which any weapon fashioned against us, shall never prosper.

Anyone who chooses to be preaching Jesus without his inseparable Mother, Mary, is only preaching a false and imported Jesus. Such a person should be greatly feared and avoided. For he is a *man of bad doctrine, a heretic, a reprobate and an anti-Christ.* The only Jesus who is the one and the only Saviour, is that one conceived, formed, born, nurtured and offered up for the salvation of the human race by the Most Blessed Virgin Mary. Wherever the Virgin Mary is, there Jesus

Christ is *Lk. 2:16; Lk. 2:35; Lk. 2:48 51; Jn. 2:1 4; Jn19:25* etc. In all spiritual and physical matters, Jesus is our *Doctor* and Mary is our *Nurse.* Jesus was not known as Jesus in heaven. He has been God from all eternity. It was after his birth by Mary that he started answering Jesus. We all know that there is nothing God does not have. But at the annunciation God was lacking in human nature. He needed this nature for Him to do His work of redemption. He had to take our nature so that He could die to redeem us. But he lacked this. So He had to beg or plead to or even pray to the Blessed Virgin Mary in order to have this nature. As the Virgin Mary accepted His plea, He became incarnate in her and was born into the world as Jesus Christ. Thus, Jesus Christ is a combination of God and Mary. That is, God plus Mary equal to Jesus and Jesus plus Mary equal to salvation. Therefore any *Christology (i.e. the study and teaching about Christ)* that is being carried out without its complement *Mariology (i.e. the study and teaching about Mary)* and vice versa results in *"Incomplete Salvation"*, but Christology plus Mariology and vice versa results in *"Complete Salvation"* or simply put Jesus minus Mary = *Incomplete Salvation* but Jesus plus Mary = *Complete Salvation.* This is the inseparability of Jesus and Mary. This is our balanced salvation equation. Anything short of this makes our salvation equation unbalanced.

Children of God, whenever a person unites himself with Mary, that person has instantly united himself with God since Mary herself is intimately united with God. And whatever prayers, petitions, praises, honour, thanksgiving and glory we offer to her, these go straight away *(i.e.*

redundantly) to God. In the gospel according to St. Luke, we find that when Elizabeth was blessing and glorifying the holy Virgin, Mary did not say anything to her other than this: *"My soul magnifies the Lord; and my spirit rejoices in God my Saviour"* Lk. 1 :45-47. Mary's response shows that she thinks nothing else but God alone. God has created her for his glory. Her soul and spirit are intimately united with those of God. *For anyone who is joined to the Lord is one spirit with him 1Cor. 6: 17.* Mary is not just joined to the Lord, she is one with the Lord-Lk. 1:28; Jn. 1:14. Hence, whenever we glorify the holy name of Mary, the glory goes straight away to God. That is to say, if we unite ourselves body and soul with Mary, with her soul, our souls will forever magnify the Lord, and with her spirit, our spirits will always rejoice in God our Saviour.

CHAPTER 12

MARY'S DIGNITY
NEXT TO GOD, HIGHEST AMONG OTHER CREATURES

In one of his divine prophecies through the prophets of old, God the Father Almighty made it known to us that Mary's dignity is a special one: that she is next in dignity after God and highest in dignity among all creatures. She is the greatest power under God. In the book of Isaiah, chapter two, verse two *(Is. 2:2)*, the Bible says: *"In days to come the mountain where the temple stands will be the highest one of all, towering above all the hills."* The Blessed Virgin is the person who is hereby symbolized in the Old Testament by this great mountain, whereas other creatures are represented by the lower mountains. The reason why she is described as the mountain towering above all other mountains is because by the dignity of her election as Mother of God, she has been raised above all other creatures. In the explanation of St. Paul about the dignity of Christ, he says that Christ was made greater than the Angels, just as his name is greater than theirs. For God has never said to any of his angels, *"You are my son; today I have become your father" Heb 1: 4-5.* In the same way, Mary was made greater than all creatures including angels and saints, just as her name is greater than theirs. For God has never said to anyone other than Mary, *"You are my mother, today I have become your son".*

The Holy Mary is the mountain above other mountains because although many people before her flourished with wonderful sanctity yet no one as to her was given the fullness of grace. Her dignity is therefore above that of all other creatures, angels and saints put together. In the gospel according to St. Luke, the Angel Gabriel addresses Mary as *"Full of grace."* This gospel context mingles revelations and ancient promises, thereby helping us to understand that among all the *"spiritual blessings in Christ"* this is a special blessing. In the Mystery of Christ, she *(Mary)* is present even before creation, as the one whom the Father has chosen to be the Mother of His Son in the Incarnation. And, what is more, the Son has chosen her, entrusting her eternally to the Spirit of holiness. In an entirely special and exceptional way, the Blessed Virgin is united with Christ Jesus, and similarly she is eternally loved in this beloved Son, Who is one with the Father and in Whom is concentrated all the glory of grace. At the same time, she is and remains perfectly open to this gift from above. According to Vatican II, Mary *"Stands out among the poor and humble of the Lord, who confidently await and receive salvation from him."*

According to the *"Dictionary of Mary,"* in the context of the

Angel's announcement, the greeting and the name *"Full of grace"* refer first of all to the election of Mary as Mother of the Son of God. But at the same time, the *"Fullness of grace"* indicates all the *supernatural munificence* from which Mary benefits by being chosen and destined to be the Mother of Christ. If this election is fundamental for the accomplishment of God's salvific designs for humanity, and if the eternal choice of Christ and the vocation to the dignity of adopted children is the destiny of everyone, then the election of Mary is wholly exceptional and unique. So also is the singularity and uniqueness of her place in the Mystery of Christ.

Mary is *"Full of grace"* because it is precisely in her that the Incarnation of the Word, the *hypostatic union* of the Son of God with human nature, is accomplished and fulfilled. As the Council says, Mary is *"the Mother of the Son of God. As a result she is also the favorite Daughter of the Father and the Temple of the Holy Spirit. Because of this gift of sublime grace, she far surpasses all other creatures, both in heaven and on earth."*

Children of God, it is Mary's *fullness of grace* and her *election as Mother of God,* that have made her the next in dignity after God and the highest in dignity among all other creatures. This has led to Elizabeth's exclamation at the sight of Mary: *"Why should this great thing happen to me, that my Lord's mother comes to visit me" Lk. 1:43.*

If I may ask, have you ever asked yourself, why should this

great thing happen to me wretched sinner, that Mary the mother of God is also my mother? Why should this great thing happen to me, that she comes to visit me in apparitions? Are you one of those who criticize Mary? Do you criticize her apparitions? If you have been doing this, please, stop it. Why not learn from Elizabeth how to humble yourself. We do not deserve to be children of Mary because she is too great to be our mother. Let us always offer thanksgiving to God for having given us his very own Blessed Mother, this woman who is next in dignity after Him, this woman who is highest in dignity among all creatures, the past, the present and the future, and above all, angels and saints put together, to be our mother also. Oh, what a precious *"Gift"* to the human family.

MARY: THE CHANNEL OF
FULFILLED PROMISES

In the Old Testament, God had made promises to our ancestors in the faith with regard to the salvation of the human race. To bring these promises to fulfillment, God had created and formed a channel in his divine mind, but kept it hidden from all men up to the time of the message of the Angel Gabriel to a Virgin, in a town in Galilee named Nazareth. Mary the Mother of Jesus is that Virgin. She is the channel through which all the promises made to man by God were fulfilled. This was the reason for Mary's Song of Praise or the Magnificat in the gospel according to St. Luke, especially with regard to this particular portion: *"Therefore, God has fulfilled the promise he made to our ancestors, to Abraham and to all his descendants forever"* Lk.1:54-55. The *Magnificat* of Mary shows that she is conscious that the promise made to the fathers, first of all to Abraham and to all his descendants forever, is being fulfilled in herself. What is that promise? It is the land promised to Abraham by God, which in the New Testament is life everlasting in heaven.

Although so many people had made sacrifices in the Old Testament including Abraham, yet these sacrifices were never considered worthy and acceptable to God for the remission of sin. When Abraham was taking Isaac his son to the Mount of Moriah, to sacrifice him to God, Isaac carried the wood on his head. As they walked along together he said to his father, *"Daddy, where is the sacrificial lamb?"* and he replied him that God will provide *Gen. 22:7.*

It is this question from Isaac that John the Baptist was answering in the New Testament, when he saw Jesus the Son of God and Son of the Virgin Mary coming to him in the River Jordan and he said to the people, *"This is the Lamb of God, who takes away the sin of the World" Jn. 1:29.* The wood that Isaac was carrying for sacrifice symbolizes the cross of Jesus Christ. The knife with which Isaac was to be slaughtered by Abraham is a symbol of all the materials for crucifixion, namely, hammer, nails etc. That sacrifice which Abraham could not perform with Isaac his son on the Mount of Moriah, Mary has performed with Jesus Christ her son on the Mount of Calvary *Gen. 22:9-12; Jn. 19:25-30.* This way, the land promised to our ancestors, first of all to Abraham and his descendants forever, is hereby inherited by Mary and Jesus, together with all faithful children of God (that is you and me), the *"descendants"* of Mary in *Rev. 12:17.*

MARY OUR CO-REDEMPTRIX
(Songs 2:2; Lk. 2:35)

Among the numerous titles given to Mary the Mother of God is the title *"Co-redemptrix."* But more important than the title itself is its doctrinal content. What does the word *Co-redemptrix* mean? It refers to Mary's cooperation in the Redemption.

1.*In the sense that she knowingly and willingly gave birth to the Redeemer. This one is called indirect or remote cooperation.*

2.*She dispenses to humanity the fruits (or graces) of the Redemption already accomplished by Christ alone. This one is called cooperation in the subjective redemption.*

3.*Besides the two types of cooperation, Mary also contributed to the Redemption itself. That is, she cooperated in the redemptive action of Christ that was consummated on Calvary. This one is called cooperation in the objective Redemption.*

 The Blessed Virgin together with Jesus Christ, atoned for our sins, merited every grace necessary for salvation, and joined the Saviour's sacrifice on Calvary to appease the wrath of God. It was in view of this joint operation of Son and Mother that God was pleased to cancel our debt and take us back to His friendship broken by sin. These facts, analyzed and clarified by the church are well rooted in the Bible.

In Song of Songs, chapter two, verse two *(Song of Songs 2:2)*, the Holy Spirit of God says, *"As a lily among thorns is my spouse among women."* The Blessed Virgin is the spouse of the Holy Spirit because Jesus Christ her son was conceived by the Holy Spirit - *Mt. 1:20; Lk.1:35.* She is said to be a lily among women because she is the one blessed among women *Lk. 1:42.* But the main reason why she is described as a lily among thorns is to prophesy about the cooperation she would undertake in the saving work of Christ, that is, the sufferings that she would pass through in the work of salvation. The thorns stand for all attacks and blasphemies against the Holy Mother of God. All the new theological doctrines aimed at destroying her image and dignity as mother of God, as well as her honour and devotions. All blasphemous names such as *queen of the coast, an envelope, an ordinary woman and the false accusation that she had other children after Jesus Christ according to the flesh.* The thorns also include such things as apostasy, *heresy, and atheism, the loss of the true faith, proliferation of churches, abortion, immodesty, materialism, bad government, injustice, occultism, inhumanity, war* and many others. These are the things, which unite together to form the thorns surrounding the immaculate Virgin Mother. This prophecy was confirmed by Simeon in the New Testament, when after dedicating the infant Jesus to God he said to Mary: *"And sorrow, like a sharp sword, will pierce your own heart"* Lk. 2:35.

Beloved child of God, assuming on a Sunday you bring your newborn baby to the church for dedication. And the choirs sing sweet songs as you walk to the altar. Then, after blessing your child and saying so many good things about him, the priest turns to you and says, *"this child will become a source of great problems to you,"* what will you tell him? Of course, you will instantly revoke such pronouncement and may even attack the priest. Some people may even go straight away to the Bishop of the Diocese, demanding for the immediate removal of the priest from the parish. While some others may revoke such pronouncement by throwing these words to the priest: *Back to sender: this is not my portion: I reject it in Jesus name: Holy Ghost fire.........etc.* Yet, Mary did not revoke the pronouncement rather she moved straight away into meditation.

The reason for this prophecy was to confirm the Virgin Mary as our *"Co-redemptrix"*, that is, she has been chosen by God to share in a special way, the sufferings involved in the saving work of Christ. God had conferred on her ever before creation as his own mother and co-worker in his plan of salvation. We will not understand this till we get to heaven to see what we owe to the Holy Mother of God, and the immeasurable graces and the heavenly bounty poured on her by Christ when he gave her to the church as a helper in his plan of salvation.

In Mary, Christ poured out his immeasurable graces and mercy to all men. She shared all his sufferings; she drank that bitter chalice that he drank to the dregs. She suffered along with him in working out our salvation. Her immaculate sorrows and tears combined with her son's sacred passions and tears to save mankind. Therefore, while Jesus has become our *"Redeemer"*, Mary has become our *"Co-redemptrix."* Everything that Jesus has merited for this work because it was strictly due to him, Mary has merited also because it was supremely fitting. And while Jesus has become our *"Advocate"* with God the Father, Mary likewise has become our *"Advocate"* with Jesus Christ her Son. Jesus is the way to the Father according to *Jn. 14:6; Jn. 2:5*, and Mary is the way to Jesus according to *Jn. 19:26-27*. No one can go to the Father except by means of Jesus, so also no one can go to Jesus except by means of Mary. Thus, if no one can go to the Father except by means of Jesus, and no one can go to Jesus except by means of Mary, it implies that no one can actually go to God except by means of Mary. This truth remains unchangeable because truth itself is God.

Children of God, Mary is chosen from all eternity, above all creatures, to be the mother of God and the mother of the church. Towards this, God entrusted in her motherly care, the church. He adorned her with every grace and virtue as *"Co-redemptrix"* and a *"Distributor"* of divine graces. He has put the world under her motherly care. Through her, abundant graces are given to all men. And the choicest title to glory that God has given to her is that of being *"Co-redemptrix"* in his plan of salvation, and at the same time, the *"Mediatrix"* of all graces.

C H A P T E R 1 3

MARY
THE THEOTOKOS OR THE MOTHER OF GOD

S aint Thomas of Villanova (Bishop) said: "*For a long time I have wondered and been at a loss to understand why the evangelists have spoken at such length about John the Baptist and the other apostles, and yet told us little about the Virgin Mary, who in life and distinction excels them all. Being at a loss, as I say, to understand this, all I can think is that it pleased the Holy Spirit that it should be so. It was by the providence of the Holy Spirit that the evangelists kept silent, because the glory of the Virgin, as we read in the Psalms, was all within, and could more truly be thought of than described. The outline of her life: that Jesus was born of her is enough to tell her whole story. What more do we seek for in the Virgin? It is enough for us that she is the mother of God. What beauty, I ask us, what virtue, what perfection, what grace, what glory does not belong to the mother of God?*

The Holy Spirit has not described her in words, but has left her to us to picture in our mind, so that we may understand that there was nothing she lacked of grace, perfection, or glory which could be imagined in the mind of a chaste human being, or rather that in fact she surpassed all understanding. So when she was wholly perfect, it would not have been right to describe her in part, for fear that we might think she could have lacked what had not been described. To say of the Virgin Mary only that she is the mother of God surpasses all that can be said under God. The Divine Maternity explains everything in her.

Someone said to me, *GregMary*, why do you Catholics call Mary Mother of God, whereas God is both *omnipotent* and *omniscient* the *Alpha* and the *Omega* the *Beginning* and the End *Rev.22:13*. God himself created Mary, how then do you call her mother of God?

In answering his question, I put this question to my protestant friend, who is Jesus Christ? And he answered that he is the Son of God but not God himself. So, I took him to the book of *Isaiah, chapter nine, verse six (Isaiah 9:6)*. Here, the Bible calls Jesus Christ 'Almighty God'. So also is the Gospel according to St. John *Jn.20:28*. Again, in *Jn.14:10; Jn. 17:11* and *21*, Jesus maintains that he is one being with God the Father. So, I said to my protestant friend, if Jesus is God, it follows that Mary the mother of Jesus, is mother of God. Finally, in *Lk. 1: 43*, the Holy Spirit speaking through Elizabeth, addresses Mary as mother of God. At this point, my good friend dropped his argument and began to honour the Blessed Virgin as mother of God.

Children of God, Jesus had one divine person and two

natures: *Divine* and *Human*. From the moment of his conception he was both God and man and from that moment, the Blessed Virgin has been Mother of God. When in her reply to the Angel Gabriel she said: *"I am the servant and handmaiden of the Lord; be it done to me according to your word"*, at that moment the power of the Holy Spirit immediately formed and generated the body of Christ from the pure blood of Mary, infused the newly created soul into that body, and united the divinity inseparably with that soul and body. This Divinity and Humanity are united in only one Person so that the actions of the Divine Nature or the Human Nature are the actions of one Person, the Divine Person. Jesus Christ is God and Man, perfect God and perfect Man, Son of God and Son of the Virgin Mary.

Since God was born of Mary, she is the Mother of God. If we could not say that she is the Mother of God, to whom she has given a body then neither could we adore this Body, nor would we have been redeemed by the sacrifice of this Body on the Cross; nor would we be united to the Divinity in receiving this Body in the Eucharist. It is impossible to deny her this title (Mother of God) without also denying the reality of the Incarnation, the Gospel truth in *Jn.1:14.* Therefore, the belief in Mary as Mother of God is linked to the belief in the reality of the Incarnation. The Divine Maternity is such a sublime privilege that no creature, not even Mary herself, can understand it fully. To understand her dignity as Mother of God in all its fullness, we would have to understand fully the dignity of the Son of God whose Mother she is. This is a mystery beyond our understanding and must be accepted in faith. Mary is truly Mother of God because *"according to the flesh"* she gave birth to Jesus Christ who was truly God from the moment of his conception. The expression *"according to the flesh"* means that she is not the source of Christ's divinity. She did not give birth to God from all eternity. But since Jesus is truly God and truly man, Mary is truly Mother of God. Hence we call her the *"Theotokos"* or the *"Mater Dei"*. The Church affirmed this belief at the Council of Ephesus in the year 431 AD. Then, at the Council of Chalcedon, in the year 451 AD, the Church stated these truths as *dogma*, that is, an article of faith, an official doctrine of the Church.

When we honour Mary as mother of God, we are actually professing our belief that Jesus Christ is truly God. We are not saying that Mary came before God. Rather, the Second Person of the Blessed Trinity Who existed from all eternity became flesh in the womb of Mary and lived among us. He is that same God that said to Moses on *Mount Sinai: "I Am Who Am" Ex. 3: 14; Jn. 8:28.*

One day, I was with a protestant pastor who was praying and covering everyone with the precious blood of Jesus. After the prayer, I asked him, *from where did you get this blood, which you pour everywhere and every time?* And he answered it is the blood of Jesus. When I took him to the letter of St. Paul to the Hebrews, we saw Jesus Christ himself saying to his Father in heaven: *"I thank you Father because you need no sacrifice rather you have prepared a body for me" Heb. 10:5.* Then, I explained to him that apart from Christ's death on the cross which is the greatest and worthy sacrifice acceptable to God for the remission of sin, the reason why he said these words: *"You have prepared a body for me"*, was to testify that he had taken his whole human nature from Mary. This was the reason for John's statement, *"And the word was made flesh and dwelt among us"* - *Jn.1:14*. This implies that the *"Precious Blood"* of Jesus is taken from the *"Immaculate Blood"* of Mary. Also, the *"Sacred Heart"* of Jesus is inseparable from the *"Immaculate Heart"* of Mary. The two Hearts are one, ever united in love. The Heart of Jesus, the Word Incarnate in Mary, is forever united to Her Maternal Heart, and both are a single entity in suffering for the redemption of the whole world.

Jesus Christ is God and God is Spirit, and a Spirit has no flesh. So, for God to redeem the world, he needed a human mother that would supply him flesh and blood, and that human mother was Mary. Jesus is the bone of her bone, the blood of her blood, and the flesh of her flesh. Thus, whenever we suddenly meet a danger and seek the defense and protection of the blood of Jesus Christ, we are simply seeking the defense and protection of the blood of Mary the blood of our salvation.

Brethren, the reality of the Divine Motherhood explains the human and supernatural perfection of Mary. It is the only case of which a *"Son"* was able to *"fashion"* His Mother as He wanted her to be. The church of which Mary is the Mother, must admire and confide in her the wonders wrought by Christ very own self. The Church must admire the beauty with which she was clothed even before original sin could stain her immaculate heart. God has chosen her as his mother and overwhelmed her whole being with graces. All the beauty and graces He poured on her are reflections of his divine perfection.

Jesus the Son of Mary is all   powerful. And according to *Dictionary of Mary*, He could not but prepare for Himself a Mother worthy of Him, a *"worthy Mother of God,"* totally devoted to her exceptional vocation: Redeemed by reason of the merits of her Son and united to Him by a close and indissoluble tie, she is endowed with the high office and dignity of being the Mother of the Son of God and, in consequence, the beloved daughter of the Father and the temple of the Holy Spirit. Because of this sublime grace she far surpasses all creatures, both in heaven and on earth.

On a similar note: *"The Father of mercies willed that the Incarnation should be preceded by its acceptance by her who was predestined to be the Mother of His Son, so that just as a woman contributed to death, so also a woman should contribute to life. This is true in outstanding fashion of the Mother of Jesus, who gave to the world Him who is Life itself and who renews all things and who was enriched by God with the gifts that befit such a role."*

Because of the *"close and indissoluble tie"* it forms between the Mother and her Son, the Divine Motherhood both calls for and explains *"the cooperation absolutely beyond compare" that Mary brings* to the work of the Saviour: a cooperation that makes her our Mother *"in the order of grace."*

As Mother of God she surpasses, in an immeasurable degree, all other creatures, Angels and human beings. They are God's servants, but she is His Mother.

We have the sublime dignity of being children of God by adoption; Jesus alone is His Son by nature. But Mary is not the adoptive Mother of the Son of God; she is His real Mother. We can lose our Divine adoption, but Mary can never lose her Divine Maternity. God might have created a more beautiful world, more perfect people, more marvelous spirits; He could not have made anything more wonderful than a Mother of God.

The Blessed Virgin is the Mother of the Son of God. She fulfills the duties and enjoys the rights of a true mother. From her own flesh and blood, she formed the Body of her Son. She nourished Him, clothed Him, and educated Him. She commanded Him and He Obeyed. How can we ever understand the great love that bound their hearts together!

As Mother of the Son of God, She is associated with the Father in the generation of His as man. What a marvelous woman, to be the Mother of her own Creator! What an amazing distinction for a woman, to have a Son in common with God. The Father loves His Son: the Mother rejoices in her Son. The Father tells His Son: From the womb, before the morning star, I begot you; the Mother says to her same Son: From the womb, I, a virgin, brought you into the world. With the Father she, too, can say: *"This is my beloved Son in Whom I am well pleased"Mt.3:17.* She is amazed at her own glory, nor can she herself understand her elevation, for by the very fact of being made mother of the Creator she became the best right Mistress and Queen of all creation. Today she is the one commanding in heaven because she is still the Mother of God in heaven as she was on earth; Jesus, who is omnipotence itself remains her son forever. And whenever she calls on him, he answers "Yes Mother."

In 1 Jn. 4:2-3, the Bible says that, *"Any man who does   n o t acknowledge that Jesus Christ came as a human being is an anti-Christ."* There are two main lessons obtainable in this biblical passage, namely:

1. *The Bible wants us to recognize and acknowledge Christ's double nature: divine and human.*
2. *The Bible also wants us to believe in Mary as Mother   o   f both God and man. Whoever does not believe this truth, also does not in anyway believe that Jesus is both God and man. Hence, he is an anti-Christ. Whatever Jesus Christ is, Mary is the Mother of that thing. No human being other than Mary contributed to Christ's human nature. She is the one and only human parent of Jesus. It is this same body of Mary that Jesus took and dwelt among us. He took human flesh from Mary in order that he could die, and he is also God in order that he could save us. In summary, the Blessed Virgin Mary is Christ Humanity on earth. Anyone who refuses to accept this fact will die eternally Jn. 8:24.*

Dear humble readers, with regard to all these facts available, you have no reason not to acknowledge and honour Mary as Mother of God. Please, go ahead and do so: for you would be professing your belief all the more that Jesus is truly God and truly Man.

The Divine Maternity itself, more than any particular privilege, is a mark of God's love for Mary. During all eternity it will be one of our greatest joys to admire this infinite love of God for her.

We should rejoice with her in the happiness that filled her heart because of such love. We can ask her to pray to God that we return His love with some of the generosity and fervor with which she loved Him.

O! Mary in whose holiest womb God was received, in this womb the record of our sins was effaced, in this womb God became Man while remaining God. He was carried in your womb, condescending to be born in the same way as we are. Yet when he was received into your arms he did not leave the bosom of his Father. God is not divided as he carries out his will, but saves the world without suffering any division in himself. When the Angel Gabriel came into your presence he left heaven behind, but when the Word of God who fills all creation took flesh within you, he was not separated from the adoring hosts of heaven. What tongue could worthily hymn you through whom we have received such magnificent blessings? With what flowers of praise could we weave a fitting crown for you from whom sprang the flower of Jesse, who has crowned our race with glory and honour. What gifts could we bring that would be worthy of you of whom the whole world is unworthy?

If St. Paul could say of the other saints, that the world was not worthy of them, what can we say of the mother of God, who outshines all the martyrs even as the sun outshines the stars.

O! Mary, you are the *Container* of the *Uncontainable* because in your most holy womb God, whom the whole creation, even the highest heaven, cannot contain, squeezed himself and was carried about. You are a woman to be admired and most worthy of every honour; a woman to be uniquely revered, wonderful above all women, the saviour of her parents and giver of life to her descendants.

I bow down before you, *resting-place* of the Divine Bridegroom, *temple* of eternal Wisdom, *sanctuary* of the Holy Spirit, *palace* of the Blessed Trinity, mother full of love and tenderness, *fountain* of beauty, *well-spring* of wonders, *golden key* of Gods kingdom, the *admiration* of the angels, and the *joy* of the human family.

O! Mary, O! God's own divine world, you are wonderful beyond all wonders. I am never more eloquent and more content than when I speak of you. Truly, he who is powerful did great things for you; truly because he made you his own mother: all generations: the past, the present, and the future must call you blessed.

CHAPTER 1 4

THE LITANY OF THE
BLESSED VIRGIN MARY

Litany is a word with Greek origin meaning "to pray," and, more specifically, "to ask in earnest." It is a Christian form of prayer centering on a series of invocations and responses. For example: "St. John," "Pray for us," "St. Paul," "Pray for us," "St. Pio," "Pray for us," etc.

Originally, litanies were short prayer petitions or invocations repeated over and over. For example: "Lord, have mercy," or "Lord, hear our prayer." Litanies were used by ancient Christians to venerate and pray to the Saints. The various litanies which are used in the church today include the Litany of the Saints, the Litany of the Blessed Virgin Mary, the Litany of the Sacred Heart, the Litany of the Precious Blood, the Litany of St. Joseph etc. Among these Litanies, our discussion shall center on the Litany of the Blessed Virgin Mary.

The Litany of the Blessed Virgin Mary was made popular by St. Peter Canisius in Italy. And because its use was attested for, from the famous Italian shrine known as Loreto, in the year 1558, it is therefore referred to as the Litany of Loreto. It was originally approved by the Church under the Papacy of the Holy Father, Pope Sixtus V, in the year 1587. The Litany of the Blessed Virgin includes the following titles of Mary, namely:

Refuge of Sinners

In Song of Songs 8:10, the Blessed Virgin Mary speaks in the words of Solomon: "I am a wall, and my breasts are the tower: since was I in the eyes of the Lord as one finding peace."

By being a wall, the Virgin Mary stands as the "Defender" of all persons who fly to her patronage. And by her breasts being a tower, she shows mercy towards her children and servants as a tower of refuge. By appearing before God as a peace maker, she makes peace between sinners and God. In this way, she becomes the "Refuge of sinners." She performs the task in the following ways, namely:

I.When on a journey a mother is leading her child by the hand and mistakenly the child falls on the way and stains himself, the mother does not abandon him in that dirty condition, rather she picks him up, runs her motherly arms over the stain and wipes it away. Then she encourages the child to continue the journey with her. In the same way, when a sinner is being led by Mary on a spiritual journey the journey to heaven, and mistakenly the sinner falls again into sin, the Merciful Virgin does not abandon him in that sinful condition as long as he has confidence in her. That is to say, when a sinner seeks for Mary's intercession with the aim of renouncing his sins and returning to God, no matter how hardened he might be, she quickly receives him with joy and love. She takes him just as he is, with his limitations, defects, sins and frailty, then each day she continues to transform him until Christ is formed in him. As she does this, at the same time, she pleads to God and calms his anger against the sinner in question. In this way, Mary becomes the "Fire Extinguisher." She continues to extinguish the fires of God's anger and chastisement against sinners and so reconciles them with God and makes them good friends again.

II. The second way by which the Virgin Mary performs her duty as the peace maker between sinners and God is this:

Mary bore two children - Jesus and sinners. She bore Jesus according to the flesh and all men or sinners according to the spirit. Like Cain who killed his brother, Abel Gen. 4:8-14, sinners killed Jesus their brother on the cross of Calvary. And their just reward is hell fire. But Mary as Refuge of sinners, full of mercy and compassion, standing and weeping before God who is the Just Judge, will plead to Him on behalf of sinners. She prays Him in His constant love and great mercy according to Ps. 51:1, to have mercy upon her His handmaid and spare the sinners. She pleads to God that since she has already lost one child (Jesus crucified), she is now left with only one child (the sinners), and although divine justice demands for their condemnation to hell fire, if this is done, your handmaid will become childless. This sorrowful appeal from Mary restrains the avenging arms of God against sinners and brings upon them divine mercy and pardon.

Children of God, just as the sick poor, abandoned by everybody because of their misery, find shelter only in charitable institutions, so do the most wretched sinners, though rejected by all, find a refuge in the mercy of Mary. For God has placed her in the world to be a shelter for sinners, a public hospital, the Refuge of sinners.

Dismas was a great highway robber, a hopeless sinner, who received salvation from God by having recourse to Mary as his Refuge of sinners. After the purification in the Temple, Mary and Joseph decided to stay in Jerusalem for nine days, in order to renew their offering of the child Jesus, and to acknowledge their gratitude to God. On the fifth day of this Novena, God instructed them to take their divine child and flee into the Land of Egypt in order to save his life because king Herod was seeking to kill him-**Mt. 2:13-15**. So, the Holy Family set out on the long and difficult journey that took them days.

One evening they arrived at the camp of some highway robbers, who were at first inclined to rob and torture them, but for the powerful intuition and timely intercession of the Blessed Virgin Mary, God turned their hearts. When the leader looked at the infant Jesus, somehow, his wicked heart was deeply touched, and he ordered his men not to harm the holy travelers. He took them into his house and ordered his wife, also a robber, to give them some food.

As the Holy Family settled comfortably in a corner, the Virgin Mary requested the woman to give her some water, in a container, to bathe her divine son. And as she bathe the infant Jesus and washed his swaddling clothes, suddenly there was a miracle: the water became clearer than it had been before. The couple were filled with awe and wonder. They whispered to each other: *"That little boy is not an ordinary child. He is holy."*

In one corner of the house lied on the floor a three-year-old boy, who was suffering from leprosy, and was abandoned to die by the parents because they didn't know what to do again, in order to save his life. The boy's name is Dismas. He was the child of this couple. The leprosy was so advanced that it covered all his face and body. The father whispered to the mother, *"to ask the Blessed Virgin to permit them, to bathe their leprous child in the water she has used. Perhaps it will heal him."* But before the woman could say a word, the most merciful and compassionate Mother urged her to bathe the child in the water, and as soon as this was done, the leprosy disappeared. The skin became smooth and shiny. The boy became healthy. The parents and their gangs of robbers were astonished. They were filled with awe and wonder, joy and gratitude. Later the Blessed Virgin had a long talk with the mother. In the end she stopped living from crime and repented of all her sins. The next morning, as the Holy Family set out to leave, the father humbly and emotionally prayed to Mary: *"My lady I beseech Thee, remember me wherever you are."* This request the Virgin Mary granted and even extended its fruit to their leprous child, who later became a thief like father and mother, and died after thirty-three years. He was one of the two thieves, crucified with Jesus on Calvary. At that time, again, by Mary's intercession in appreciation for the charity done to her by his parents (thirty-three years ago) he was given the grace for perfect contrition. Thus, he acknowledged his faults and confessed his sins. In the end he said to Jesus: *"Lord, remember me in your heavenly kingdom."* This request Jesus granted: *"Today, I promise you, you will be with me in paradise"*-Lk. 23:40-43. Dismas was 36years at the time and Jesus was 33. The name of the other thief is Gestas. This one was unrepentant

Children of God, the lessons we can draw from this story include the following:

1. By the charity of the highway robbers inspired by Mary, multitude of their sins were covered and wiped away.

2. By their confidence in Mary and recourse to her as Refuge of sinners, salvation was given to them.

3. The little boy who later became a thief, had at first suffered from physical leprosy, and was healed by Mary's presence and prayers. Then at the hour of his death, again, by Mary's presence and prayers, he was healed of leprosy of the soul which was his sins. He has since become a Saint: the first Saint ever in Christendom to have been canonized and by Jesus Christ Himself on Calvary. Today, the Church refers to him as Saint Dismas the Good Thief.

But what makes him a good thief? Can a thief ever be referred to as good? Yes because by Mary's intercession his sins are forgiven. He is reconciled with God and is now a good thief. All these facts prove that Mary is truly "Refuge of sinners."

Dismas is the model and patron Saint of all criminals- all highway robbers: all undertakers. So then, my brother, my sister, are you a thief? Are you a criminal? Do you want repentance? You, too, could also become a good criminal. Run to Saint Dismas the good thief, he will help you.

Beloved Christian souls, always have recourse to Mary. She cannot reject you on account of your sins. Rather, the more wretched you are, the greater the claim you have on her protection because God Himself has made her the Refuge of the most forsaken. Do not despair, O sinners. Go with confidence to Mary. You will find her hands filled with grace and mercy, and open to you. She is full of sympathy, and more anxious to help and assist you than you yourselves can be. She is the fountain open to all sinners, the fountain for the washing of sinners -**Zech. 13:1.**

Oh, how many sinners have found God and have been saved by thy means O Mary. Please, do not allow me to perish in my sins. Continue to pray for us sinners, now, and at the hour of our death, Amen.

ARK OF THE COVENANT

Covenant is a sacred and loving relationship or agreement between God and humanity. The term Covenant is derived from the Latin word *"Convenire"* meaning *"come together"*, *"one mind"*, and *"an agreement."*

In ancient times covenants were agreements *(something*

like business contracts) between two or more parties. Such covenants or agreements were finalized and confirmed through sacred rituals and ceremonies. The Holy Scriptures reveal that the ancient Hebrews agreed to a spiritual covenant friendship with God, which was more than a mere business deal, and was to last forever. It was an agreement, offered by God *(or Yahweh)*, that would be rooted deeply in a mutual sense of relationship, love, and respect. Some of the great figures associated with these covenant agreements include Abraham, Noah, and Moses. In the covenant agreement, God promised to cater for his chosen people, the Israelites of Old, provided they kept his commands *Ex.19:5-6; Ex. 24:4-8.* And whenever the people chose to jeopardize the original covenant relationship through sinful choices and alliances, great misfortune and sorrow befell them.

In the covenant agreement, the Jewish people during the time of Moses were given divine commandments written on the two tablets of stone. The covenant was carried in a box often called the *"Ark of the Covenant."* The Ark became necessary, since it was the only sacred means devised by God, to dwell and communicate with his people. For they all had sinned and fallen short of his glory and could no longer encounter him directly *Rm. 3:23.* The Ark with all covenant materials always had God's presence and majesty. For example, when the Ark crossed the River Jordan, wonders happened the water suddenly stopped flowing

Joshua 4:1-7. But when God later found faults with the Old Covenant *(because the people had fallen away from their covenant faithfulness),* he promised to change it with a new and lasting one *Heb. 8:7-13.*

In the New Testament, God replaced the Old Covenant with a new and lasting Covenant, which is Jesus Christ, to perfectly set people free from the wrongs they did while the Old Covenant was in force *Heb 9:15.* This is God's greatest covenant with humankind. It all started when the Angel Gabriel, came to Mary and asked her to be the Mother of the Son of God. With faith Mary replied: *"I am the Lord's servant, may it happen to me as you have said" Lk. 1:38,* a reply so sweet to the hearing of God and so fortunate for mankind. At that moment, the Holy Spirit overshadowed her and Jesus was conceived in her womb. At this juncture, Mary became the *"Ark"* carrying the New Covenant *(Jesus Christ)* and the first *"Tabernacle"* of the New Testament. For if Jesus Christ the Son of God and Son of the Virgin Mary is the New and Everlasting Covenant, then Mary whose most pure womb he dwelt in and was carried about, is the *"Ark"* of the New Covenant.

As the Old Ark was made of precious and incorruptible wood, containing the staff of Aaron the high priest, the tablets of the law and the manna of the desert, which was regarded as the Seat of God and the Safeguard of the children of Israel, so is the New Ark made of the Virgin

Mary, who is immaculate and incorrupt, and bore within her most pure womb, not merely the staff of Aaron, but Jesus Christ who is the High Priest himself, not merely the tablets of the law but the Divine Legislator himself, who is the fulfillment of the Law and the Living Bread that came down from Heaven, and is the Protection of all Christian people, the Israelites of the New Testament *Heb. 9:3-4; Jn. 6:51-58.*

Just as King David arose and went to the *"hill of Judah,"* in order to bring the Ark of old to Jerusalem **2** *Sam 6:1-3; 1 Chr. 13:5-6,* so also Mary the new Ark arose and went to the house of Zechariah, in the *"hill-country of Judaea"*, in order to visit Elizabeth *Lk. 1:39-40.*

As king David leapt and danced with joy because of the coming of the Ark of old into Jerusalem *2 Sam. 6:5; 1Chr. 13:8,* so also John the Baptist leapt and danced with joy in the womb of Elizabeth because of the coming of Mary the new Ark into their house *Lk. 1: 44.* And just as David exclaimed with a loud cry and said, *"How can the Ark come to me now?"* - *2 Sam 6:9; 1 Chro. 13:12,* so also, Elizabeth exclaimed with a loud cry and said, *"Why should this great thing happen to me, that my Lord's mother (i.e. Mary the New Ark) comes to visit me?"* *Lk 1:43.*

While the Ark of old stayed three (3) months in the house of Obed Edom, and the Lord blessed Obed and his family *2 Sam*

6:11, 1 Chr. 13:14, so also, Mary the new Ark stayed three (3) months in the house of Zechariah, and the Lord blessed Zechariah and his family and filled them with his Holy Spirit *Lk. 1:56.* Elizabeth was even blessed with the gift of prophecy *Lk. 1: 41-42.* And Zechariah was able to speak again as he too was blessed with the gift of prophecy *Lk. 1: 62; Lk. 1: 67-80.* John the Baptist was also blessed by being baptized and consecrated in the womb of his mother, and was born immaculate *(but was not conceived immaculate). While Zechariah means "the Messiah will come", John means "the Messiah has come", and* Elizabeth means the "Lord has remembered his promise".

In the Old Testament, just as the Ark of the Covenant performed wonders, so also Mary the new Ark performed wonders, not only like the Ark of old, but in a sense, more than it. Whenever the Israelites of old took the Ark to a battle, they came back victorious *Joshua 6: 1-26; Num 31:1-12.* So also, whenever Mary the New Ark battles with the deadliest enemy of the children of God called Satan or the red dragon, she defeats him and crushes his head to pieces and the result will be total victory for all Christian people, the Israelites of the New Testament *Gen. 3:15; Rev. 12:1-6* and *13-17.*

Now let us consider the account of John the Evangelist, who interpreted the Bible according to the tradition and formation he received from Judaism, as he compares the

Old Covenant given to Moses on Mount Sinai to the New and Everlasting Covenant, which is Jesus Christ. This consideration offers an immediate parallel between Moses and Jesus: *"For while the law was given through Moses, grace and truth came through Jesus Christ" Jn. 1:17.* Jesus is the new Moses, bearer of a new covenant and source of a new order of grace and truth. His work is the introduction of a new economy, or new people of God.

Jesus is the one person who fulfilled and extended through his work of salvation, the original covenant relationship between God and all of humanity. This new covenant relationship promises life and a holy friendship with God forever, if we fundamentally accept the proclamations of Christ, follow him, and live in accord with the values and challenges of his gospel.

Furthermore, according to St. John, the sign of Cana is explicitly a *manifestation* of Jesus' glory: *"Jesus manifests his glory and his disciples believe in him" Jn. 2:11,* just as God (or *Yahweh*) had manifested his glory on Sinai *Ex.24:16-17* and accredited Moses as his prophet *Ex 19:9.*

In rabbinic tradition, wine is a common symbol for the Mosaic Law and the teaching of the Messiah. Thus, the mention of the *"six stone water jars"* prescribed for Jewish ceremonial washings in *Jn. 2:6,* could well be an echo of the purification ordered by God (or *Yahweh*) prior to his manifestation to the Israelites of old: *"They must wash their clothes and be ready for the third day..." Ex. 19:10 11* and *14 15; Ex. 24:5-8.* And obviously, God manifested Himself to the people on the third day *Ex.19:16 25; Ex. 20:18-21.*

The words of Mary to the servants *"whatever Jesus tells you, do it" Jn. 2:5*, correspond perfectly to the words of the people promising to adhere to the covenant: *"We will do everything that the Lord has said" Ex 19:8; Ex 24:3* and *7; Deut 5:27.* By making use of the words of the people declaring their adherence to the Sinaitic Covenant, Mary becomes the representative and personification of the Messianic people. By her total receptiveness to the words of her Son, she expresses the faith of the whole Messianic people disposed to receive the revelation brought by Christ. Hence the more reason why Jesus addressed her as *"woman"* in *Jn. 2:4; Jn. 19:26 27*, a symbolic name often applied to the Jewish people *Ezk. 23:2; Isaiah 54:6; Hos. 2:4; Jer 3:1* and *20.*

By pointing the way to Jesus as in *Jn. 2:5*, Mary begins to play a role in the creation of the new people of God, the Messianic Community that will form around Jesus as in *Isaiah 66:7-10; 1 Pt. 2:9-10*, and be ruled by him as in *Rev. 12:5.*

Children of God and Mary, we have all seen how John has integrated his *"account"* with the *"Sinaitic Covenant."* It is here that the most original and most profound experience of ancient Israel, finds its peak and completion. Jesus appears as the Prophet preeminent, the bearer of a definitive revelation, symbolized by the new wine in *Jn. 2:9-10*, of better quality than the old. Jesus is the new Moses, promised and awaited: *"I will send them a prophet like you from among their own people; I will tell him what to say, and he will tell the people everything I command"* Deut 18:18; Acts 3:22.

At this juncture, we can conclude with the Dictionary of Mary that *"The manifestation of the glory of Jesus, at Cana, is not only the crown and recapitulation of Israel's experience. It also has the force of a beginning: it inaugurates the properly Messianic Age and effects the transition to an absolutely new economy, at the same time, it points to the coming of the supreme Hour of glorification through the cross."*

While the old Covenant was sealed on Mount Sinai *Ex 24: 5-8*, the new and everlasting Covenant was sealed on Mount Calvary *Jn. 19:25 30*. Mary's presence at this great hour was specifically willed by Jesus Christ her Son in order that he might make with her, but one same sacrifice and be immolated to the Eternal Father by her consent, just as Isaac of old was offered to the will of God by Abraham's consent. This is how the new and everlasting Covenant was sealed *Heb. 13:20*. The most sacred ritual activity by which the Church of Christ, the Holy Roman Catholic and Apostolic Church, expresses her belief in and celebrates this new and everlasting covenant as instructed by Jesus

Christ himself is the Eucharist or the Holy Mass. To this effect, St. Paul says, "For I received from the Lord the teaching that I passed on to you: that the Lord Jesus, on the night he was betrayed, took a piece of bread, gave thanks to God, blessed it, broke it, gave it to his disciples and said, *"This is my body, which is given for you. Do this in memory of me."* In the same way, after the supper he took the chalice and said, *"This chalice is God's new covenant, sealed with my blood: the mystery of faith, which shall be poured out for you and for many for the forgiveness of sins. Whenever you drink it, do so in memory of me"* 1 Cor. 11:23-25; Mt. 26:26-28; Mk 14:22-24; Lk 22:17-20.

Jesus is the new *"Covenant"* and Mary is the *"Ark"* of the new covenant. What the old Ark could only signify, and solely in a purely local way, Mary the new Ark makes a reality, and in a personal way; she is an effective sign of God's presence with His people. And in heaven, she is always hailed as the Ark of the Covenant. No wonder when the temple of God in heaven opened and showed the Covenant Ark **Rev. 11:19,** which in turn released some flashes of lightning, rumblings and thunder, an earthquake, and heavy *"hail"* as in *Lk. 1:28,* there was a sudden appearance of the Blessed Virgin Mary in her glory and splendour *Rev. 12:1.* By being the new and everlasting Ark of the Covenant, Mary closes the Old Testament and opens (or begins) the New Testament. She is the living Ark of the Covenant. Hence we honour and hail her in the litany of Loreto: *"Ark of the*

Covenant, Pray for us."

Just as in the Old Testament, God instructed Joshua and the Jewish people to carry the image of the Ark of the Covenant and march in procession round the city of Jericho, the enemy of the chosen people of God, and in the end, Jericho walls were demolished by the invisible hand of God and the people were captured and conquered, so also, we the Israelites of the New Testament, carry about the statue of Mary, the new and everlasting Ark of the Covenant and march in rosary procession, asking God who dwells more magnificently and more divinely in Mary, to fight for us against all our **"enemies"** symbolized by the **"walls"** of Jericho. During this spiritual exercise, the power of God in the statue of our Blessed Mother, does for us what the image of the Ark of Old did for the Israelites of old, and even much more than that. That is, God through His New Ark, crushes Lucifer and all his agents to pieces, solves our problems both spiritually and materially, and clears the way for us his new chosen people.

This same spiritual exercise of the Jewish people during the time of Joshua is also evident in the Catholic Church in this form or manner. During the celebration of the feast of Christ the king which is done throughout the Catholic world, the Priest or Rev. Father carries a monstrance containing the Eucharist and as he takes the lead, the faithful children of the church line behind him and they all march in procession, singing, praising, thanking and adoring God, in the same way as the Israelites of Old, led by David, offered thanksgiving to God, praising his most holy name, singing and adoring Him because of the coming of the Covenant Ark into Jerusalem *2 Sam 6: 13-15; 1 Chr. 13:8.* Today, during this spiritual exercise, the Rev. Father takes the place of David or Joshua the high Priest, the Monstrance containing the Eucharist takes the place of Mary the New Ark, whereas the Eucharist which is Jesus Christ himself is the New and Everlasting Covenant. This is so because, Jesus Christ has not come to abolish the old law, rather he has come to fulfill it. He alone is the *"Fulfillment"* of the old law *Mt. 5: 17-19.*

In spite of all these facts, rooted in the Bible, analyzed and clarified by the church, some people still go about refusing to acknowledge Mary's indispensable position in the economy of salvation. And they go about helping the red dragon, attacking and blaspheming her most holy name. It is high time we stood up to tell these people, these *"anti Marys"* and *"anti Christs"*, that our mother Mary who is truly the Ark of the Covenant, is the means to go to Jesus and that whoever neglects her, is bound to perish in his sins and will be damned forever. She deserves total reverence and honour from all creatures, both human and angelic. If God could be so angry as to strike Uzzah (whose intention was not even bad, but to prevent the Ark from falling and damaging) to death for touching the Ark of Old in *2 Sam 6:6 -*

8; *1 Chr. 13:* *9-11,* on the grounds that he did not show enough reverence to it, what then do we think would be the penalty in store for those who not only show irreverence to our Mother Mary, who is the living, the new and everlasting Ark of the Covenant, but actually attack her and blaspheme her most holy name? *He, who says his father should not kill him and neither should his mother kill him, let him not kill himself.*

Those who claim to have received Jesus yet continue to reject his Blessed Mother, should better have a rethink. For since the Covenant and its Ark are inseparable, Jesus and Mary are inseparable. No one can reach out to the Covenant (Jesus) without first of all passing through its Ark (Mary). There is no place in the Bible, beginning from Genesis to Revelation, where the ancient Hebrews carried about the old covenant without its inseparable Ark. As the old Ark was used in carrying about the holy presence of God, so does Mary, the new Ark, carry about the holy presence of God. She is the *"Gate"* of heaven and the *"House"* of God. And wherever she is, there, the blessings of God flow in the highest. For example:

When the image of the Ark of the Old Covenant was kept in the house of Obed, God blessed the entire family because; they kept it with reverence and devotion-*1 Chr. 13:13-14;* and *2 Sam 6:12.* So also, in every family where the statue of the Blessed Virgin is kept with utmost reverence and devotion,

God blesses the family.

The Blessed Virgin Mary is the true Ark of God symbolized also by the Ark of Noah in the Old Testament *Gen. 6:14; 8:19.* For while the Ark of Noah was the instrument used by God, for safeguarding the earthly life of the human race, the Blessed Virgin is the instrument used by God, through Jesus Christ her Son, for safeguarding the eternal life of the human race.

And just as the Ark of Noah floated on the waters that were inundating the earth; the Blessed Virgin floated on the waters of concupiscence and sin, which were inundating the souls of men.

Children of God, the coming of the Son of Man is imminent. It will be like what happened in the time of Noah. On that fateful day of the flood, people were still eating and drinking up to the very time Noah went into the boat; only those who entered the boat were saved. So also, on the day of the coming of the Son of Man, only those who would take refuge in the Blessed Virgin, shall be saved-*Mt. 24.:37-39;Lk.17:26-27.* In other words, just as the earth was re-peopled by those who took refuge in the Ark of Noah; so also, Heaven would be peopled by those who take refuge in the Virgin Mary. Therefore, let everyone now enter into the safe refuge of the Immaculate Heart of Mary; the spiritual Ark of this end of times. She alone is the Ark that goes to

Heaven. Jesus Christ her son is the captain of this most beautiful Ark. Tomorrow may be too late. A word is enough for the wise.

Health Of The Sick:
In *Prov. 3: 16-18*, the Bible addresses the Blessed Virgin as *"Health of the sick"*. In the confirmation of this, the Bible says: *"Length of days is in her right hand, and in her left hand riches and honour. She is the tree of life, and health of the sick to them that embrace her, and happy is everyone that retains her."*

Mary is said to be the tree of life because Jesus Christ the fruit of her womb is life *Jn. 1:4; Jn. 14:6*. She is called the health of the sick because, in her fullness of grace, she can obtain both spiritual and physical health and life for those who seek her intercession. She obtains spiritual health or life for those who seek her intercession and are burdened with sins. She also obtains physical health or life for those who seek her intercession and are physically unhealthy or dead. Yes, because Jesus the fruit of her womb is the Author of both spiritual and physical life - *Jn. 10: 10; Jn. 11:25*. Children of God come and let us carry all our sicknesses to Mary, the Health of the sick. Let us not deny her the glory of saving our lives, as well as solving our problems, both spiritual and physical.

Virgin Most Faithful: In the book of *Wisdom 10: 13 - 14*, the

Bible says: *"She forsook no one even when He was sold. She never left Him until she had helped Him regain His power and become the ruler of all the people that once oppressed and persecuted Him. And she made it known that He was falsely accused, as she helped Him regain His eternal honour".*

Although this passage of the Bible talks about how Joseph the son of Jacob was led by wisdom when he was sold by his brothers to the Egyptians, but later became the ruler of all of them as was destined by God. The whole truth of the matter is this: *Joseph was only a symbol of He who was to come Jesus the Saviour, whereas wisdom itself symbolizes Mary the Seat of Wisdom the Virgin Most Faithful.* She did not forsake anyone, even the most hardened sinner, when Jesus Christ her Son was sold by his own disciple, Judas Iscariot *Lk 22: 4-6; Mk 14:43 - 45.* And when everyone abandoned him, even his own disciples *Mk 14:50*, she never left him rather she remained faithful and followed him all through. She shared in his sufferings, helped and consoled him, and even prayed for all men. And when eventually she saw him die on the cross *Jn 19:25 - 30*, resurrect and ascend into heaven, to sit at the right hand of the Father, which was his eternal hounour *Lk. 24: 1-2 and 51; Mk. 16:19*, it became known to everyone that he was falsely accused, as he now rules over all the people that once persecuted and crucified him *Rev. 19:13 - 16.*

Virgin Most Prudent: The Blessed Virgin Mary speaks in

these biblical words: *"Prudence is mine: strength is mine: by me kings reign and princes decree justice" Prov. 8:14 15.*

The word *"Prudence"* means acting only after careful thought or planning. Mary is truly the Virgin Most Prudent because she alone possesses perfect prudence. This is evident in *Lk. 1:29*. When after receiving messages of salvation from the Angel Gabriel, she questioned him and waited for his answer so that she might judge prudently whether the messages agreed with what the prophets had said about the Messiah, and with the principles of her religion in order not to make mistakes. She knew that not every spirit should be trusted until after a test *1 Jn. 4:1.* For the angel of darkness sometimes disguises himself as an Angel of light, as was the case with the first woman, Eve *Gen. 3: 1-13; 2 Cor. 11:14.*

Mary is the Most Prudent of all that God has created (and those that He is yet to bring into existence) because she alone is full of grace. She alone teaches perfect prudence, temperance, justice and fortitude which are the most profitable virtues in life - *Wis. 8:7.* That the Bible says she was deeply troubled at the first hearing of the Angel's voice, does not imply that she was afraid or unworthy of such honour, as some non-Catholics have been saying, rather she only reflected and wondered out of humility and deep faith, as she recalled her pious practice of perpetual virginity not until the Angel made her to understand that she would not loose her virginity as she would only become pregnant by the power of the Holy Spirit.

Mother of our Saviour: In the book of *Jer. 14:17*, the Bible says: *"Let my eyes shed down tears day and night, and let them not cease, because the virgin daughter of my people is broken with a great affliction, with a very grievous blow."*

Mary is the Virgin Daughter of the Most High God. She is said to be broken with a great affliction, because Jesus Christ her Son is unjustly tortured and crucified and she shared in a special way all the sufferings involved in this saving work. Her immaculate sorrows and tears combined with her Son's sacred passions and tears to save mankind. Hence we call her our *"Co-redemptrix"* and invoke her in the Litany of Loreto as *"Mother of our Saviour."* Even Simeon the high priest testified to this when he told Mary that she would suffer great affliction to the point that the pains would break her own heart *Lk. 2:35*. Mary is the woman whose offspring is the Saviour of mankind. Therefore, she is honoured and invoked by the title *"Mother of our Saviour."*

Seat of Wisdom: In its explanation of Mary as the "Seat of Wisdom," the Bible says: *"It is she that teaches the mysteries and the knowledge of God"* *Wis. 8:4*. To the unwise she says, come in, ignorant people." *Prov. 9:4*, and listen to what you are taught. Hear my instructions and be wise and do not reject it *Prov. 8: 32 33* because I speak with a gentle *"wisdom" Prov.31:26.*

Yes, the Blessed Virgin Mary speaks with a gentle wisdom. There is nothing that she teaches the children of God other than the knowledge of God and how best to do his will. She did it at the wedding of Cana, when with a gentle wisdom, she said to the servants: *"Whatever Jesus tells you, do it"* Jn. 2:5, that is, whatever is the will of God, do it. This is a woman with whom Jesus spent the whole of 30 years (plus 9 months in the womb) of his 33years on earth, in privacy or in hiddeness. Oh, who can tell what transpired within this period of hidden life between Jesus and his Blessed Mother? He gave her this much and gave 3years to the rest of the other creatures, you and me. Who can tell what he was teaching her within those years of hidden life? Then in Lk. 2:48, Jesus said to Mary: *"Did you not know that I must be in my Father's house?"* Also in Jn. 2:4, Jesus said to Mary: *Did you not know that my hour has not yet come?"*

The two phrases "Did you not know" imply that Mary actually did know. Therefore, these phrases give significance to the fact that she is the Seat of wisdom. There is no wisdom more than doing the will of God. By Mary's obedience to the word of God, as well as her election as mother of Christ who himself is the *"Divine Wisdom"*, She becomes the Temple of Divine Wisdom, or the Tabernacle of Divine knowledge, or the Seat of Divine Wisdom.

Mirror of Justice: In the book of *Prov. 8: 20-21*, the Bible says: *"She walks in the way of justice, in the midst of the paths of judgment, that she might enrich them that love her, and fill their treasure. She is the brightness of eternal light, the unspotted Mirror of God's majesty and the Image of goodness"* *Wis.7:26*. She stands on the right of God's throne to intercede for sinners in time of judgment *Ps. 45:9*

Yes, Mary is truly the Mirror of God's divine justice because she possesses all the merits and virtues divinely expected of all men to acquire, in order to gain entry into the kingdom of heaven. It is in her that God has recovered his image and likeness which had been seized by Satan. She is the *masterpiece* of God's creation and the *reflection* of his divine perfection. She is the **"Model"** that anyone wishing to enter into the kingdom of heaven must look up to. In all truth, Mary is the *"Mirror of Justice."*

Mother of Good Counsel: With regard to this Marian title, the Bible reads: *"Counsel and Equity is mine"* *Prov.8:14.* Therefore, listen to me children and accept my **"counsels"** so that you will be happy *Prov. 8:32*, for by wise counsel, you will conquer your enemies in battle *Prov. 24:6*.

It is evident at the wedding of Cana that Mary is the Mother of Good counsel. She counseled the people to do the will of God always and as they accepted her good counsel, they were rewarded with the best wine *Jn. 2:8 10*. In this way too, the Blessed Virgin goes from one country to another, counseling her children on how best to do the will of God and win victory against the evil one so that they, too, may be rewarded with the best wine which is life everlasting in heaven e.g. Fatima, Lourdes, Nigeria etc. Thus says St. Bonaventure: *"Give ear; O ye nations; and all you who desire Heaven, serve, honour Mary, and certainly you will find life."*

Cause of our Joy: The Blessed Virgin Mary as prefigured by Judith, appears as the cause of the joy of all God's people, the past, the present and the future, in the form: *"Thou art the joy of Israel"* Judith 15:9, for the Lord has clothed you with salvation and victory. Therefore, let your children rejoice Is. 6:10.

The Blessed Virgin is truly the "Cause" of our joy because with joy, we see her become the Virgin Mother of the Word who becomes man in her most pure womb. Her Son Jesus Christ is born of her to become our Saviour and our Redeemer. In Him alone all humanity have the possibility of being set free from slavery to sin, to join in a communion of life and love with the heavenly Father.

Virgin Most Powerful: Here the Bible reads: Yea, the first "Power" shall come, the kingdom to the daughter in Jerusalem Mic. 4:8, and so shall she possess the "Power" and "Wisdom" of God Wis. 7:25, and with this, she shall convey souls into God's friends Wis. 7:27. By grace, she has become the highest power under God. She is filled with the power of God the Father, covered with the Holy Spirit, and carried in her womb God the Son *Lk. 1:35*. God therefore, has conferred on her the Trinitarian abidingness, indwelling and empowerment, making her all-powerful.

Virgin Most Amiable: Here the Bible reads: "She was exceedingly fair, and her incredible beauty, made her appear *"Agreeable"* and *"Amiable"* in the eyes of all" *Esther 2:5*, and the king himself (i.e. God) desires her *Ps. 45:11*. Her ways are beautiful ways, and all her paths are peaceful *Prov. 3:17*, and her conversation has no bitterness, or her company any tediousness, but joy and gladness *Wis.8:16*.

Mother Undefiled: Here the Bible reads: "My dove, my **"undefiled"** is but one **Songs 6:9.** Therefore, *"no defiled thing"*, cometh unto her" *Wis. 7:25*.

The Blessed Virgin Mary is honoured and invoked in the Litany of Loreto as Mother Undefiled *(i.e. without sin or sinless Mother)* because she is full of grace *Lk. 1:28*. She was conceived and born immaculate so as to better co-operate in the saving work of Christ. All through her life, she contracted no sin, neither original nor actual. And when it was time for her to bring the Son of God into the world, she conceived him by the power of the Holy Spirit. She conceived virginally, gave birth virginally, and remained an undefiled virgin unto death. Oh, the Blessed Virgin is truly

"Mother undefiled."

Mother Most Admirable: Mary's incomparable beauty results in the following words of admiration of her: *"How beautiful art thou, thou art all fair my love, thy eyes are dove's eyes, thy lips are as a scarlet lace and thy speech so sweet Song of Songs 4:1-3. O daughter, thy head is like Mount Carmel and thy hair like purple. How fair and how pleasant art thou, O love, for "Admiration" Song of Songs 7: 5-6.*

This is the same woman whose incomparable beauty made all women, including queens and concubines, look at her and praise her. With her incomparable beauty, King Solomon was moved to exclaim in ecstasy: "Who is she that cometh forth as the Morning Rising, fair as the Moon, bright as the Sun, terrible as an Army set in battle array?" *Song of Songs 6:8 -10.* Oh, the Holy Mary is truly "Mother Most Admirable."

Holy Virgin of Virgins: The Blessed Virgin is hereby shown in the Bible as the Holy Virgin of Virgins: *"Many daughters have gathered riches, thou hast surpassed them all" Prov. 31:29.* **There are many virgins without number, but my dove, my holy one is but one. All the other virgins, including queens and concubines looked at her and praised her" Song of Songs 6: 8-9.**

The Blessed Virgin is said to have gathered riches more than all other women because Jesus Christ (who is the greatest of all riches) is the fruit of her womb. Again, because God exempted her from all stain of sin, the Holy Spirit chose her out of all the other virgins as his only beloved and holy one, *"My dove, my holy one is but one."*

Tower of David: In the Litany of Loreto, Mary is honoured and invoked by the title *"Tower of David."* To confirm this fact, the Bible reads: *"Thy neck, O daughter, is like the Tower of David, round and smooth, with a necklace like thousand shields round it"* Song of Songs 4:4.

By being the Tower of David, Mary protects and defends all her descendants in *Rev. 12:17*, who through Jesus Christ, have also become the descendants of David. She protects them against the attacks and snares of the enemy called Lucifer or Satan or the red dragon.

Tower of Ivory: In the Litany of Loreto, Mary is honoured and invoked as *"Tower of Ivory."* With regard to this, the Bible says: "Your neck is like the *Tower of Ivory*. How beautiful you are, how comely the delights of your love"- *Song of Songs 7:4 and 6*.

My dear people of God, in the litany of Loreto, the titles given to our Blessed Mother are many. I cannot continue to list them all. The much I have listed and explained here, it is my prayer, should be able to enrich you all.

C H A P T E R 1 5

MARY
THE WOMAN ALL GENERATION MUST CALL BLESSED

In the Old Testament, God speaking through the mouth of king David, promised to make Mary's name be remembered by all people and decreed that all generations must call her blessed: *"O daughter, I will make thy name to be remembered in all generations: therefore, all the people shall bless thee forever and ever"* Ps. 45:17.

Then in the New Testament, Mary herself attested to the above promise made to her by God: *"From now on all generations must call me blessed."*- Lk. 1:48. This divine promise is being fulfilled in her in that, apart from being exempted from all stain of sin, both original and actual, God has also placed her in a position that can never be equaled by any other person in all human experience, and indeed, in all creation. That position is her election as mother of God *(i.e. Her Divine Maternity)* and the source of salvation to the human family. Hence whenever the word *"Salvation"* is mentioned, the name *"Jesus"* is remembered and adored by all creatures in heaven, on earth, and beneath the earth *Philippians 2:10*, and whenever Jesus is mentioned, with joy, the name *"Virgin Mary"* is remembered, honoured, praised and blessed by all creatures - the past, the present, and the future *Lk. 1: 42; Rm. 16:6; Prov. 31: 31*. This is God's own divine eternal decree.

Children of God, no matter what people may say, no matter what they do, whether some people have chosen not to call Mary blessed, what cannot be denied is the fact that the Most Holy Trinity, the Church, the Holy Bible, the Heavens, Myself and all generations have continued to proclaim her blessed and this is forever. Everything will pass away but God's proclamation of Mary's perpetual blessedness must remain because God's own words will never pass away *Mt. 24:35*. Consequently, whoever decides not to honour Mary is deciding not to do the will of God and will face the consequences of such decision. He shall be destroyed and forgotten forever *Hosea 4:6*. But those who bless and honour Mary, whether in terms of the recitation of the Hail Mary, or in terms of the recitation of the Holy Rosary and other Marian Prayers, shall be abundantly rewarded with heavenly graces. If God could say to Abraham who is quite inferior to Mary in the order of grace: *"I will bless you and make your name famous, so that you will be a blessing. I will bless those who bless you. But I will curse those who curse you. And through you I will bless all the nations"* *Gen. 12:2-3*, what then do we think He (God) has said to Mary when He called her "Full of Grace?" Obviously, the Magnificat of Mary has become the song that will make her name famous and be remembered forever. It is in her that all that God has said to Abraham were fulfilled. For by means of Jesus Christ the fruit of her womb, God has blessed all the nations. Whoever that curses her, shall be cursed by God. But whoever that blesses and honours her as his mother, shall be blessed with great wealth and long life which is life everlasting in heaven *Ecclesiasticus or Sirach 3:3-6*.

Now let us examine how Jesus Christ himself has honoured and glorified Mary by his actions and words. Apart from his *"obedience"* to her at the wedding of Cana and at his finding in the temple, as well as his address of her as *"woman"* (both at Cana and at the foot of the cross), a symbolic name often applied to the Jewish people, let us consider his glorification of her in the gospel according to St. Luke.

MARY: THE WOMAN
GLORIFIED BY CHRIST

In *Lk. 11:27*, a woman spoke up from the crowd and said to Jesus: **"Blessed is the woman who bore you and nursed you."** This woman filled with the Holy Spirit is hereby toeing the line of other persons in the Bible whom the same Spirit has used to glorify Mary. And the scripture is urging everyone to follow suit. The Bible wants us to understand that the immeasurable graces and the heavenly bounty with which God has adorned the Blessed Virgin, are such that all those who let themselves be formed and nursed by her, are certain of acquiring great wisdom about the kingdom of heaven. Hence they are certain of their salvation. For they would be appearing agreeable before God, since the Holy Virgin will always and richly feed them with those merits and virtues that make her God's number one always e.g. *Faith, Chastity, Love, Wisdom, Prudence, Charity, Obedience, Meekness, Endurance*, and above all, *Humility Prov. 8:32*.

Although Jesus' reply to the above observation reads thus *"Rather, blessed are those who hear the word of God and obey it" Lk 11:28.* Yet it is not contrary to what the woman has said of Mary. If I may ask, who out of all that God has created, the past, the present, and the future, has perfectly kept the word of God? It is no person other than the Blessed Virgin. Or did she, who believed by faith and conceived by faith, who was the chosen one from whom Our Saviour was born among men, who was created by Christ before Christ was created in her did she not do the will of God?

Indeed the Blessed Virgin certainly did the will of God. It was for her a greater thing to have been Christ's disciple than to have been his mother, and she was more blessed in her discipleship than in her motherhood. The happiness of first bearing in her womb he whom she will obey as her master was her own.

She is the only one who kept the word of God in *excelsis*, that is, in the highest. For when the Angel Gabriel brought a message of salvation to her, she accepted it whole heartedly and resigned herself to the will of God: *"Behold, the handmaid of the Lord! Be it done unto me according to your word"* Lk 1:38. When God asked her to sacrifice this Son of hers to His will on the cross, again, she resigned to it. With regards to these considerations, we can see that Mary perfectly kept the word of God more than any other creature. Thus, the reply made by Jesus in *Lk. 11:28* to the observation in *verse 27*, was not meant to contradict or brush aside the Holy Spirit inspired praises, heaped on his Blessed Mother by the woman. Rather, it proclaimed, attested, confirmed and completed them. Obviously, Jesus wanted the woman (and in a sense, all of humanity) to learn and understand the fact that Mary is not just blessed because of her election as Mother of God, but also because she believed the word of God in *excelsis Lk. 1:45*.

One other important lesson of this great event is that, by his actions and words, Jesus proclaims the glories of his mother the *"Glories"* of Mary. For the woman that glorified Mary, did so because of what she heard and saw Jesus Christ her Son do. This implies that all true imitators of Christ, you and me, the Christians, should by their actions and words, proclaim the glories of Mary the Mother of all Christian people. That is, our actions and words should reflect the life and virtues of Mary to the extent that people will not find it difficult to attest that we are truly her children and servants and that she is a good woman, worthy of emulation. In other words, our actions and words should be such that we would be able to lead those souls with whom we come in contact, to a renewed devotion to Mary. Hence all generations shall call her blessed.

Now let us consider what Saint Paul has to say about honouring and glorifying Mary.

MARY: THE WOMAN GLORIFIED
BY ST. PAUL

In the letter of St. Paul to the Romans, he emphasizes on the need for us to honour, thank and glorify Mary the Mother of Our Lord Jesus Christ. In *Rm. 16: 6* St. Paul says: *"Greetings to Mary who has worked so much for mankind."*

St. Paul honours and glorifies Mary in emulation of the Eternal Father, who first of all, honoured and glorified her through the Archangel Gabriel in *Lk. 1:28.* By his actions and words, St. Paul proves wrong all those who argue that any human greeting, honour, praise or worship, directed at the Blessed Virgin results in idolatry. All generations must deeply honour and glorify Mary because by means of her, salvation has been given to mankind. Again, what the Holy Spirit says of her: *"All generations must call her blessed"* Ps. *45:17* and *Lk. 1:48* implies honour and worship.

With reference to the *Dictionary* and a book titled *"Honouring or Worshipping Mary"*, written by Msgr. Pro. F. C. Okafor, the term *"Worship"* in its context implies deep admiration and respect shown to, or felt for somebody or something. Therefore, to worship Mary is to express our deep admiration of and respect for her, in imitation of God who himself, was the first to worship her. Yet some people continue to condemn the idea of worshipping and honouring her on the grounds that it militates against the worship and adoration given to God.

My Question: If Magistrates and other people of high ranks are honoured with the address of *"worship"*, for instance, a magistrate is addressed as *"your worship"*, is a magistrate greater than Mary the Mother of God? Of course no.

Therefore Mary, the woman in whose womb God-whom the universe and indeed, all creation cannot contain, squeezed and dwelt for nine months, worthily deserves honour and worship. Mary should be worshipped by all mankind because in her, God has recovered his image and likeness which had been seized by Satan. She alone is full of grace, that is, she is sinless or perfect in everything, whereas all other persons have sinned and fallen short of God's grace *Rm.3: 23*. She is the *"Master piece"* of God's creation and the true *"Reflection"* of His divine perfection.

Children of God, the term *"worship"* differs greatly from the term *"adoration"* which is the homage and the worship strictly reserved for God alone. The reverence or worship accorded to God alone is above that which is accorded to his Mother Mary, Saint Joseph, Angels and Saints, and is known as *Latria*. This is a Greek word meaning Adoration. The reverence or worship accorded to Mary is above that which is accorded to Saint Joseph, Angels and Saints, and is known as *Hyperdulia*. This is a Greek word meaning Supreme Veneration. The reverence accorded to Saint Joseph who kept the secret of Heaven (i.e. Mary's mysterious pregnancy) is above that which is accorded to Angels and saints, and is known as Protodulia meaning Veneration before others. The reverence which is accorded to Angels and Saints is known as *Dulia* meaning ordinary veneration. So then, make no apology to anybody by saying: *"We are honouring Mary............ We are not worshipping her"*, for such is uneducated and uninformed. Rather, let us all join the Angels and Saints in heaven, in singing praises, giving thanksgiving, honour and worship to Mary the woman worshipped and glorified by God himself. She is the one to whom honour is due. No one other than God can honour her enough. To honour her is to be honoured by her, Angels and Saints, and above all, God himself. We should always be ready to serve her, for that is the greatest honour one can possibly receive from God. We should not be discouraged by those non-Catholics (and even some uninformed Catholics) who accuse us of practicing idolatry and giving to Mary the honour and reverence due to God alone. For if on the judgment day, this would be the only sin God will accuse us of, then it is a good and holy sin. I would be prepared to die committing such a sin. And if after judgment my reward is hell fire, I will be bold enough to say to God: My Lord and my God, since it is your will that I should follow in your footsteps according to *Mt. 11:29*, it is fitting that you should first of all, receive such a reward and I will follow suit, because you were the first to honour and worship Mary, your Mother and mine.

Children of God, honour Mary with the last breath in you. Serve her with the last drop of your blood. Don't be discouraged because of the insults and abuses people are heaping on you, the truth is that, you are doing the will of God. After running the race, we shall count the mileage. Continue to do the will of God. Strive hard in the service of his Mother despite obstacles on your way, despite your humiliations and persecutions. These are meant to prepare you for eternal glory. Do you not know that *servants of Mary (of which I am an unworthy one) always appear little to others, but great to her? They will even be despised and persecuted by many, but in their soul, they will always have her joy.* You should not feel incapable or tired of doing some Marian work given to you rather you should appreciate God and thank Him for counting you worthy of such sacred position. I tell you, *"You are highly favoured. You are already reigning with Mary in heaven".*

Whenever you find yourself incapable or tired of doing some Marian work given to you, on the grounds that it is too hard for you, the truth is that you no longer love the heavenly Mother. He, who no longer loves the Queen of Heaven when he must suffer greatly for her, has never truly loved her rather he has only loved himself in the favours and consolation she obtains for him. Please do not refuse to suffer, for you would be refusing to love. To suffer is to love. The more you suffer, the more you love. So then, my dear brothers and sisters go ahead and suffer for the Holy Virgin. You would be glad you did.

Now let us consider this question: *Does Mary the Queen of heaven lead souls to reign with her in heaven?* My answer is in the next page.

C H A P T E R 1 6

SHE LEADS SOULS TO
REIGN IN HEAVEN

In the Holy Bible, it is stated that no one other than Jesus is the Saviour of mankind *Jn. 14:6; 1 Tim. 2:5; Titus 2:13.* As a result, some people have argued that Mary the Mother of God cannot save.

Beloved brothers and sisters, although Mary is not the Saviour of mankind, her election or power as mother of the Saviour (i.e. her fullness of grace) makes it possible for her to save, especially those who humbly and confidently seek recourse to her. In the Court of Heaven she stands at the right hand of her Son Jesus Christ who is the Judge of mankind, so that by her favour and intercession, souls may be pardoned and come to reign in heaven **Ps. 45:9.**

My Question: Who is there that is saved? Who is there that reigns in heaven?

My Answer: According to Denis the Carthusian, they are certainly saved and reign in heaven for whom Mary Queen of Mercy intercedes.

In *Prov. 8:15*, Mary herself confirms the answer: *"By me kings reign"*, that is, through her favour and intercession souls reign, first in this mortal life by ruling their passions, and so come to reign eternally in heaven, where all are kings according to *Ps. 45:15-16*. And since she is the Mistress of Heaven; there she commands as she wills, and admits whom she wills. Thus St. John Damascene says: *"To serve Mary and be her courtier (a courtier is a person who attends at the court of a sovereign), is the greatest honour we can possibly posses; for to serve the Queen of Heaven, is already to reign there, and to live under her commands, is more than to govern. But those who do not serve her will not be saved; for those who are deprived of her help are also deprived of that of her son (Jesus Christ) and of the whole court of Heaven."*

MARY: THE MEANS TO
RECEIVE JESUS

Because the world was (and still is) very unworthy and incapable of receiving Jesus the Son of God directly from the Father, God devised but one and only perfect means by which it would receive him. That means or channel is shown in the prophecy of Isaiah. In the book of Isaiah, Chapter nine, verse six (Isaiah 9:6) the Bible says: *"Unto us a child is born, unto us a son is given: and the government shall be upon his shoulder: and his name shall be called Wonderful Counselor, The Mighty God, The Everlasting Father, The Prince of Peace."*

My Question: Who is this noble woman that gave us this Omnipotent child?

My Answer: It is she whom the Angel Gabriel asked to be the Mother of the Son of God in *Lk. 1:30-33*. It is the Virgin Mary, the Noble Queen of Peace. For when the Angel Gabriel came to her, he did not say the Lord is with the world because the world was not worthy of him. Rather the Angel said to Mary, the Lord is with thee so that through her the world might receive Him who created all things. She is the tree whose fruit brings peace.

This implies that no one other than the Most Holy Virgin Mary is the means devised by God for us to receive His only

Begotten Son, Jesus Christ. Mary alone is the royal road of the Saviour. Therefore, for anyone to receive Jesus in his fullness, and for Him to reign in his life as Prince of Peace, the person has to receive the Blessed Virgin first of all in her fullness, and allow her to reign in his life as Noble Queen of Peace. For she alone is the means through which God gives His Son.

MARY: THE IMMACULATE CLOUD

In the book of Isaiah, chapter nineteen, verse one *(Isaiah 19:1)* the Bible predicts that Mary would appear in the form of light or immaculate cloud, to carry Jesus the Lord and lead him to Egypt: *"Behold, the Lord will ascend upon a light cloud, and will enter into Egypt, and the idols will tremble at his presence, and the people of Egypt will lose their courage."*

In the explanation of St. Ephraim, the Lord who would appear as man in the world was Jesus Christ. He would be carried as if upon a light cloud, that is, upon the immaculate and virginal arms of Mary into Egypt.

Beloved brothers and sisters, Ephraim's explanation is correct because Mary who is described as cloud is of flesh, and because she is a virgin conceived and born without sin, she becomes light also. And upon her immaculate and virginal arms, she carried the Lord Jesus Christ and fled to Egypt, when Satan in the person of Herod wanted to kill him *Mt. 2:13-14.* This is the interpretation of the prophecy of Isaiah, chapter nineteen, verse one.

MARY SEARCHES FOR THE LOST

In the gospel according to St. Luke, when the boy Jesus was lost in the temple, Mary searched and found him after three days *Lk. 2:43-52*. This does not mean that Jesus actually got lost; for he can never be missing road in the world he himself created. Rather, the event was meant to reveal parts of the role Our Blessed Mother would play in the saving work of Christ. She is the one whose duty is to search and find all the lost children of God (you and me) who are still wandering in this terrifying wilderness. She performs the task in the following ways, namely:

a. *By means of her exemplary life on earth.*

b. *By means of the true teachings and doctrine of the church.*

c. *By means of her various apparitions all over the world e.g. Fatima, Lourdes, Nigeria, La Sallette, Mejugorje etc.*

Yes, Mary can search for us by means of apparitions because God approves of such. For example, Christ died, resurrected and appeared to Mary Magdalene by means of apparition *Jn.20: 14-18*. Again, he also appeared to his disciples by means of apparition *Jn. 20:19-23; Mk. 16: 12-18*. At the transfiguration, Moses and Elijah appeared by means of apparition *Mt. 17:3-4*. Brethren, apparition is defined as sudden but remarkable appearance of the spirit of a physically dead person (i.e. the spirit of someone who has left this world). These Biblical facts, serve as enough lessons for those who don't believe in the reality of apparitions.

In all her apparitions, the Blessed Virgin Mary unveils the plans of the red dragon against the children of God, and so helps them out of such traps. In her motherly love and care, she counsels them with these words: *"Whatever Jesus tells you do it" Jn. 2:5.*

Finally, if Mary could search and find Jesus in the temple, where will she find you? Is it in the house of Satan or in churches where there is no God? Will she find you at all? As for me, she has found me, and like Jesus, I will forever remain obedient to her, to grow in body and in wisdom, gaining favour with God and men *Lk. 2:52.*

SHE IS THE MEANS FOR
DIVINE NOURISHMENT AND TRANSFORMATION

In the book of *Song of Songs 5:1*, the Holy Spirit of God says: *"I have entered my garden, my sweet heart, my spouse: I have eaten my honey; I have drunk my wine with milk: eat, O friends; drink yea, drink abundantly, O beloved."*

The Blessed Virgin Mary is the sweetheart and spouse of the Holy Spirit. Her immaculate heart is symbolized as the heavenly garden in which the Holy Spirit dwells to make us become perfect images or true reflections of Christ who himself invites us as his friends and beloved ones, and asks us to accept his mother as our own true mother in *Jn. 19:26-27*, in order that she might nourish us abundantly with her *merits and virtues*, and above all, with *effusions of divine grace*, which are symbolized as *honey, wine and milk.*

SHE IS SURROUNDED
BY WILD BEASTS

In *Song of Songs 4:8*, the Holy Spirit of God says: *"Come with me from Lebanon my beloved spouse, come from the dens of the lion, from the mountains of the leopards."*

The Blessed Virgin Mary is the beloved spouse of the Holy Spirit. According to Richard of St. Laurence, she is said to be crowned with wild beasts, lions and leopards, that is, she is surrounded by sinners who by her favour and intercession, have been reconciled with God, and have become glorious stars of paradise, shining brightly on the head of this Queen of Mercy, and shown to St. John in the form of twelve stars in - *Rev. 12:1.*

THE BOW OF ETERNAL PEACE OR THE
RAINBOW OF THE NEW TESTAMENT

In the book of *Rev. 4:3*, St. John looked up to the sky and saw a rainbow surrounding the Throne of God in heaven. This rainbow is an expressed figure of the Blessed Virgin Mary according to *Ps. 45:9*. She is there on the throne with God not only as the Queen of heaven but also as the Mother of Mercy, in order that in her fullness of grace, she may soften God's judgment and sentence against sinners, that is, she mitigates the punishment due to you and me. It is this rainbow expressed in the figure of the Virgin Mary in the New Testament, that God meant in the Old Testament when He promised Noah that He would place it in the clouds so that whenever He looks at it, He will remember his Covenant and Eternal Peace with the human race *Gen. 9 :13-15*. That is to say, when God now looks at Mary, the *Rainbow of the New Testament,* and hears her prayers and intercessions on behalf of sinners, He instantly remembers the New and Lasting Covenant He made with mankind through her, and so pardons the sinners, forgives their sins, and grants them His eternal peace. The New and Lasting Covenant that God has made with mankind through the Holy Virgin, is Jesus Christ the Son of Mary, crucified on the cross for sinners. By this, God has replaced the Old Testament Rainbow with Mary. What the Rainbow of the Old Testament could only signify, and solely in a purely local way, Mary makes a reality, and in a personal way; she is an effective Rainbow of the New Testament. That is, a sign of God's Divine Mercy with humankind. Thus, the reason why God has not destroyed the world today, this sinful humanity, you and me, this generation whose sinfulness is far beyond that of Sodom and Gomorrah, this wicked generation, is because Mary is in heaven pleading to Him on our behalf.

KING DAVID FLIES TO HER PATRONAGE

In *Psalm 86 : 16*, the Bible confirms that all those who live under the protection of the Virgin Mary are certain of their salvation. For although the Virgin Mary was not yet born at the time of king David, David was able to obtain the mercy and pardon of God, as well as his salvation, by praying to him as a dedicated child of Mary: *"O, turn unto me, and have mercy upon me: give thy strength unto thy servant, and save the son of thy handmaid."* King David did not know what he was actually saying in this prayer, for he was completely under the influence of the Holy Spirit.

If I may ask, who in the Bible is the handmaid of the Lord? Of course, it is no person other than Mary who responded to the Angel Gabriel: *"Behold, the handmaid of the Lord! Be it done unto me according to thy word"* Lk. 1:38.

Beloved children of God, if King David could obtain his salvation from God because he humbly abandoned himself to the patronage of Mary, we all should emulate him by humbly seeking our own salvation from God, as sons and daughters of Mary, the Handmaid of the Lord. If her name alone could lead David to heaven while she was yet to be born, what do you think will become of those who seek her recourse now that she is born, and standing on the right of the throne of God in heaven according to *Ps. 45: 9?* Of course, she will protect them all the more and also lead them gloriously into the kingdom of heaven.

In *Mt. 2 :13-15,* when the enemy, or Satan, or the red dragon, in the person of King Herod, wanted to kill the infant Jesus (our eldest brother), Mary protected and defended his life in

Egypt. This was done to confirm Mary's power, wisdom and mercy, with which to protect all true children of God against the malice and subtle snares of the evil one the enemy of the cross of our salvation. This way, she becomes our *"Protectress."* She protects us both physically and spiritually.

To achieve this salvific task, the all-powerful Virgin provides us with these all-conquering weapons: the Rosary and Scapular, and asks us to always fly to her patronage and undertake consecration to the safe refuge of her Immaculate Heart. Oh, she is truly our Protectress. We should always run to her patronage like David.

With the church, let us always offer this prayer to Mary: *"We fly to thy patronage, O holy mother of God, despise not our prayers in our necessities, but deliver us from all dangers, O ever glorious and Blessed Virgin"*, amen.

C H A P T E R   1 7

THE ANGELUS

The Angelus is a prayer recited to the Blessed Virgin Mary in appreciation of God's love and mercy to pass through her, to come to redeem man. The prayer nourishes us with the joy and peace of the Good News. It refreshes our minds with the joyful account of events of the Incarnation as was brought to us from heaven by God's *Ambassador Extra-ordinary*, the Archangel Gabriel. This is the greatest thing that can happen in all human experience, and indeed, in all creation. The Angelus is biblical in character. Its biblical account goes like this:

V. *The Angel of the Lord declared unto Mary,*

R. *And she conceived of the Holy Spirit*
       - Lk. 1:30-35

V. *Hail Mary, Full of Grace...*
       - Lk. 1 : 28: 41 42

R. *Holy Mary, Mother of God........*

V. *Behold the handmaid of the Lord.*
R. *Be it done unto me according to your word- Lk. 1:38*

V. *Hail Mary.......*
R. *Holy Mary.......*

V. *And the Word was made flesh,*
R. *And dwelt among us. Jn. 1:14*

V. *Hail Mary............*
R. *Holy Mary............*

V. *Pray for us, O holy Mother of God,*
R. *That we may be made worthy of the promises of Christ.*

Others...............................Amen

With regard to this account, we could see that the Angelus has a simple structure: *announcement of the Angel; response of Mary; Incarnation of the Word.* Thus, we can say that the Angelus is in a way the story of the Hail Mary.

The present form of the Angelus was gradually attained. At first, it was recited solely in the morning. In the year *1269*, Brothers of the Franciscan Chapter of Asisi, Italy, exhorted the faithful to greet the Blessed Virgin with a Hail Mary and recall the Mystery of the Incarnation at the ringing of the bells. While at the same time, *Brother Bonvesin* of Riva *(c.1260-1315)*, introduced the evening ringing of the Angelus or Hail

Mary bell at Milan and its environs.

Little by little, this devotion became widespread in the whole of Christendom. *On October 13, 1318,* the Holy Father, *Pope John XXII* approved the custom of reciting the Hail Mary at the curfew hour. Then on *May 7, 1327,* he wrote his Vicar General at Rome to have evening bell of the three Hail Marys rung, even in the Eternal City.

In *1456, Callistus III* prescribed the daily ringing of the bells of the Angelus at midday. This devotion was highly practiced by *King Louis XI* of France. He had the *"Angelus of Peace"* rung at midday. Upon hearing the bell, the saintly king would dismount from his horse and kneel down to pray. He practiced this devotion with total commitment.

Finally, in the year 1724, the various devotions of the Angelus acquired the unitary form in which it is recited today. This was approved by *Pope Benedict XIV.* While approving the Angelus, the Holy Father prescribed that during Easter Time the Angelus be replaced by the Regina Caeli.

In the Apostolic Constitution on Devotion to Mary (*Marialis Cultus,* no. 41), *Pope Paul VI* strongly recommended preserving the custom of reciting the Angelus three times daily (morning, noon, and evening). Thus, we can conclude that the Angelus is a brief *contemplation of the mystery of the Incarnation, a faithful invocation to Mary, and an offering of our day to God.* We must not fail to say this prayer every day.

C H A P T E R   1 8

MARY
HIDDEN IN REBECCA

In the book of Genesis, chapter twenty-seven *(Gen.27)* we have four prominent persons representing four other great persons. They include Isaac, Rebecca, Esau and Jacob. Isaac stands for God the Father, Rebecca prefigures Virgin Mary, Esau stands for all the reprobates (i.e. all those who reject moral truths and have trusted in their own strength to reach God), whereas Jacob prefigures Jesus Christ and all the predestinate (i.e. all spiritually adopted children of God and Mary).

In this mysterious event, these four prominent persons make up the human family, in the same way as God the Father, the Blessed Virgin Mary, Jesus Christ and all the predestinate and in a sense, the reprobates make up the family of God.

While Jacob was totally dependent on his mother's grace and intercessions for all his needs, Esau was totally dependent on his own strength alone for all his needs. Jacob stands for all those who humbly go to God by means of Mary, whereas Esau stands for those who proudly believe in going straight - away to God on their own. While Jacob always honoured and respected his mother Rebecca, Esau paid little or no attention to her, but had always honoured and respected Isaac, their father.

Brethren, Jacob and Esau form the two types of characters we have in the world today, with regard to the worship and adoration of God our Father. Although Isaac had previously granted the request of Esau, he did so because as a good father, he was to accommodate and tolerate all his children. In the same way, in the household of God, the heavenly Father accommodates all of us and tolerates our weaknesses pending when He will reward all men according to their deeds. He considers the fact that if the prayers of those in the figure of Esau are not answered, as those in the figure of Jacob, the Esaus will vandalize His precious possession which is the souls of the Jacobs. Hence He accommodates and tolerates both Esaus and Jacobs.

Now when Isaac wanted to shower his true blessings, he asked Esau to prepare some meat for him to eat as usual, after which he might bless him. So Esau ran straight - away into the bush to fetch the meat requested. But Rebecca being a woman who knew what pleases her husband, and who always thought good of her children as a good mother, wanted the blessings be transferred to Jacob. She instructed Jacob to bring her two kids (i.e. two young goats), for her to prepare them on his behalf, to the taste of Isaac, his father. These two kids represent our bodies and souls which the Blessed Virgin Mary (who knows the true taste of God), is constantly asking of us, her obedient and humble children, to bring to her *(by means of tender love, total abandonment and consecration to her immaculate heart),* for her to prepare them to the taste of God our Father. Just as Rebecca was constantly by the side of Isaac, her beloved husband, so is Mary, the beloved Spouse of the Holy Spirit, constantly by the side of God in heaven - *Ps. 45:9.*

When Jacob, feared being discovered by his father, he became worried about the possibility of getting his blessing. But his mother, Rebecca, counselled and encouraged him with these words: *"My son, follow my counsels and fear not",* that is, by confidently following the counsels of our Mother, Mary, we shall all obtain God's mercy, grace and blessings, and find our way into his Kingdom. This is evident at the wedding of Cana. Mary counselled the people (and in a sense, all of us) with these words. *"Whatever Jesus tells you, do it Jn. 2:5.* Rebecca who knew that God had ordained it, even before Esau and Jacob were born inside her womb, that Esau should serve Jacob, understood what she did - *Gen. 25:21-26.* Jacob did not know but Rebecca and Isaac knew.

Now having deliciously prepared the two kids, Rebecca took out Esau's own best cloth and clothed Jacob with it. She then put the skins of the two kids on him, poured her very own mother's perfume on him, and asked him to take the meat to his father.

Esau's own cloth, which was given to Jacob, implies his blessings transferred to Jacob. That is to say, the blessings of those who reject and dishonour Our Blessed Mother, Mary, will be transferred to those who receive and honour her on the last day. The goat skins with which Jacob was also clothed represents Mary's garment or scapular which we wear about the neck immediately after being consecrated to her immaculate heart. Rebecca's perfume symbolizes Virgin Mary's merits and virtues, which she graciously pours on us, her children, so that we may appear agreeable before God, our Father. For those who receive and practice her virtues are blessed *Prov. 8:32*.

When Jacob got to his father, he presented him the meat. On scenting the beautiful perfume with which Jacob was dressed, Isaac cried out in a loud voice. *"Behold, the pleasant odour of my son, is like the odour of a field which the Lord has blessed" - verse 27*. That is, as we appear before God, clothed with the merits and virtues of Our Lady, He will welcome us in gladness and say: *"Behold the souls of my perfectly sanctified children. They are like the plants which the Immaculate Heart of my Mother, Mary, has cultivated."*

Again, just as Isaac acknowledged the fact that Jacob was quick in getting the meat he requested for: *"How did you find it so quickly, my son?" verse 20*, so shall it be with the children of Mary on the last day. That is, with Mary, the grace with which we can please God and gain entry into his kingdom comes very quickly.

Note: Esau who usually wasted no time in the bush could not return up till this time, why? This is because it had become difficult for him to find an animal. So shall it be with those who reject and dishonour Mary. No matter the rate at which they shout the name of Jesus. No matter the miracles and wonders they perform with the name of Jesus. The question is this: which Jesus are they doing all these things in his name? Is it the one born and nurtured by the Blessed Virgin? As we go about searching for the answer to this question, the gospel truth about this whole matter is this: These Esaus will always find it very difficult to reach God. They will continue to search in the wilderness for an animal (i.e. grace of God) until we all, the Jacobs, have gone to rest in the everlasting happiness of heaven.

Now having finished eating the meat brought to him by his son, Isaac touched Jacob and said: *"The voice is that of Jacob, but the body is that of Esau. Whether you are Jacob or Esau, I am blessing you, for now is the hour."* In the same way, on the last day, God will say to all those who practiced true devotion to Mary: *"whether you had been sinners or not, I am blessing and receiving you all into my heavenly kingdom. For by means of my Mother Mary, you have been graciously interceded for, cleansed of your sins, and clothed with her merits and virtues. And since she has even clothed you with her own garment or scapular which is the garment of salvation, you are qualified to stay here with us and enjoy the benefits of salvation."*

Jacob, in being humbly obedient to their mother, Rebecca, gained her graces and thus gained everything from their father, Isaac. That is, we all, in being humbly obedient to our mother, Mary, will gain her grace, and thus gain entry into the kingdom of heaven. In other words, we, beloved to Mary as Jacob to Rebecca, would be led by Mary to obtain so many blessings from God, as Rebecca led Jacob to obtain all the blessings he has today. This is how those who seek their salvation from God as sons and daughters of Mary are received and rewarded by God. But Esau, in being proudly disobedient to Rebecca, lost her graces, and thus, lost their father's blessings. That is, the reprobates, in being proudly disobedient to Mary, would lose her graces, as well as the Kingdom of God. This is how those who prefer to go to Jesus Christ directly on their own, and like Esau consider Mary less important, are received and rewarded by God.

While those in the figure of Jacob would receive eternal honour, those in the figure of Esau would receive eternal damnation. That is, life for the Jacobs, death for the Esaus. For God has said: *"Jacob I have loved, but Esau I have hated" Rm. 9:13.*

Just as Isaac decreed that Jacob will rule Esau forever *verses 32 - 40*, so shall we, together with Jesus our eldest brother, rule in the kingdom of God forever.
Finally, Rebecca, by her cares and power protected and defended Jacob when Esau wanted to kill him *verses 42-45*. That is, the Blessed Virgin, by her cares and powers, protects and defends all her children from the attacks of the red dragon and his human agents. This is the interpretation of *Gen. 27.*

C H A P T E R 1 9

DEVOTIONS AND MARIAN DEVOTEES

D evotion is a term taken from the Latin devotio, for *"vow"* or *"total dedication."* It describes piety or spiritual focus in general or deep reverence for the holy in prayer. Whenever we talk about devotions, we usually refer to prayers, rituals, spoken formulas, or physical gestures, used in private or with others, to worship God, to honour Mary and the Saints, and, in some way, to seek divine help.

In the ancient times, the practice of devotion had already been carried out. No wonder St. Clement of Rome, St. Ignatius, and other early church leaders spoke to Christians about prayer and ritual expressions handed down from the time of the apostles. Devotion is designed for and could be used by virtually any ordinary church member, whether in private or in communal settings, to meet one's spiritual needs.

Christian religious devotion is a free and voluntary focus on God and others in the spirit of the gospel. Thus says St. Thomas Aquinas, *"It is a virtue by which a person is inspired to worship the Creator and then dedicate everything in service to God and the world."* All devotions whether private or communal, must be genuine and have the ultimate goal of fostering spiritual closeness to God. All genuine devotions must be in harmony with the Church's doctrines and traditions. For many years, the following devotions have become the more popular Catholic communal practices, namely: *the exposition of the Blessed Sacrament, Benediction, the Way of the Cross, the Angelus, and the recitation of the Holy Rosary, Litanies, Novenas and Candle burning.* Of all these devotions, our discussion shall centre on Marian Devotion and Devotions.

Marian Devotion and Devotions

Devotion to Mary is the ardor to serve her, the better to serve God, whereas the acts by which we express this devotion are what we call devotions to Mary. In the practice of devotion to Mary, one is called to a total dedication of self to her service. Mary is the Woman most blessed of God, associated by Him in the work of the Son to an extraordinary degree, and even now sharing in His risen glory. She is for us a *"Sign"* according to **Is.** *7:14* and *Rev. 12: 1-2.* Yes because our relationship to her, says something about God, and something about ourselves. At the Council of Ephesus, the Church was led to say something about her, in the intent to say something about

Christ, who himself is God.

Throughout the history of the Church, Mary is the one who has summoned all to give praise to God *Lk. 1:46 - 55* and to practice devotion to Christ *Jn. 2:5*. While at the foot of the cross she shows the heights that fidelity must reach, even as Jesus Christ himself commands all to practice devotion to her likewise *Jn. 19 : 26 - 27*. Then in the Upper Room, she indicates how prayer tends above all to ask for the Spirit and to gather the community of believers *Acts 1:14*.

Children of God, with regards to these considerations, we could see that there is a great link between Mary and God and how inseparably one they are: *that the practice of devotion to Mary implies better devotion to Christ and to God.* That is, we devote ourselves with joy to the service of God and the church.

Veneration and love for Mary lead to God and redound to His glory, as we can see in Mary's response to St. Elizabeth's veneration and love for her: *"My soul magnifies the Lord; and my spirit rejoices in God my Saviour" Lk 1: 46 - 47*, as if to say, "Blessed are You, O Lord, in the honour that we render to the Blessed Virgin Mary".

When we invoke the Holy Name of Mary, we are actually acknowledging the fact that within the communion of saints she occupies, after Christ, the highest place and the one that is closest to us and also unites herself to Christ who according to *Heb. 7 : 25 "lives forever to intercede for us."*

Finally, devotion to Mary means to better cooperate in the apostolic mission of the Church. Thus says the Council: *"The Virgin in her own life lived an example of that maternal love by which all should be animated who cooperate in the apostolic mission of the church for the regeneration of human beings"* (LG 65). We can and should count on Mary for help to make our activities more Christian and fruitful because, having been assumed into heaven, with her maternal charity she cares for us (the brothers and sisters of her Son) who are still on our earthly pilgrimage until we are led into the happy homeland, which is heaven. We should venerate her and commend our life and apostolate to her maternal care. This is what it means to be devoted to Mary.

Now let us examine and analyze who and who are the devotees of Mary. How can we distinguish true devotees from false devotees?

The Devotees of Mary

In the practice of devotion to Mary, some devotions are true while others are false. Who therefore, is a true or false devotee of Mary? To answer this question, let us examine and analyze the following points as listed by my lovely St. Louis Marie Grignion De Montfort, namely:

A. The True Devotees: A true devotee of Mary is a person whose devotion is built on tender love. That is, he gives himself wholly and entirely (i.e. body and soul) to Mary without reserve. Like Jesus Christ, he listens to Mary and obeys her in everything, everywhere, and at every time. True devotees of Mary include the following:

Tender Devotees: These include all those whose devotion comprises of confidence, simplicity, trust and tenderness. They rely on the Holy Virgin for all their needs, both spiritual and material. They offer her all that they have including their bodies and souls. They are ready to die for her.

Interior Devotees: These are the people whose devotion comes from their very hearts. Their devotion flows from the love they have for Mary and the high esteem with which they uphold her greatness. Interior devotees can never compromise their devotion for any reason, no matter the obstacles.

Holy Devotees: The holy devotees of Mary include all true devotees of her. They persevere to avoid sin and to imitate the virtues of the Holy Virgin.

Constant Devotees: They are those who truly live by their devotion even at the greatest temptation. And when mistakenly they fall into sin, they quickly rise again by seeking recourse to the divine Mother. They show a lot of fidelity towards their devotional obligations or duties. They are constant in their devotional practices.

Disinterested Devotees: They are those whose devotion is not based on selfish interest, but to receive Christ in his fullness and be transformed into Him. They do not seek themselves but only God, and through Mary. They do not serve the Empress of heaven because of what they would gain from her, but because she deserves to be served. They do not serve her because they want to avert one danger or the other, but because she deserves every service, both human and angelic. They love her not because she obtains favours for them, but because she is worthy of love.

In all truth, all true devotees of Mary are true imitators of Christ. They are the new Jacobs. They are like trees planted by the rivers of water *Ps. 1:3; Jer.17:8; Ezk. 47:12; Is. 44:4 and Rev. 22:2..* Hence they bring forth fruits in due season. With the Blessed Virgin, their salvation is secured. They are the great saints to be formed by the Most High God with His Holy Mother. And they shall surpass most of the other saints in sanctity, as much as the *"cedars"* of Lebanon out-grow the little *"shrubs."* They are to form the apostles of this end of times.

These great souls, full of grace and zeal, and shown to king Solomon in *Songs 6:10* as soldiers of Mary, shall be chosen to match themselves against the enemies of God, who shall rage on all sides. They shall be singularly devout to Mary, illuminated by her light, strengthened with her nourishment, led by her spirit, supported by her arm and sheltered under her protection, so that they shall fight with one hand and build with the other. Yes they shall fight with one hand and build with the other. For with one hand, that is, their *faith*, they shall fight, overthrow and crush to pieces, *the heretics with their heresies, the modernists with their modernism, the fundamentalists with their fundamentalism, the atheists with their atheism, the apostates with their apostasy, the protestants with their Protestantism, the schismatics with their schisms, the Pentecostals with their Pentecostalism, the idolaters with their idolatries, and above all, the sinners with their impieties.* With the other hand, that is, their *grace*, they shall build the temple of the true Solomon and the mystical city of God, which according to *Isaiah 66: 7-10*, is the Blessed Virgin Mary the Mother of Jesus Christ, who is the true Solomon and the Incarnate Wisdom. In other words, by their words and examples, they shall draw the whole world to *"true devotion"* to Mary. This shall bring upon them many enemies, but shall also bring many victories and much glory for God alone. This is what the Holy Spirit, the inseparable Spouse of Mary, seems to have prophesied in *Ps. 59:13-14: "Then everyone will know that God rules in Israel, and that his rule extends over all the earth. My enemies will return in the evening, and will suffer hunger like dogs as they go round about the city."* This city which men shall find at the end of the world to convert themselves in and to satisfy their hunger for justice according to *Ps. 87:3*, is the Most Holy Mary, who is the House of God and Gate of Heaven. It is in this city, that is, in the Blessed Virgin, dwells the source of all blessings *Ps. 87 : 9.* For she alone is given the *"fullness"* of grace *Lk 1:28* and she alone is the *"Mediatrix"* of all graces.

In summary, all true devotees of Mary are true reflections of hers. They should be greatly followed and emulated. We should embrace them. Their docility is incomparable.

B. The False Devotees: A false devotee of the Blessed Virgin Mary is one whose devotion has no tender love. He does not give himself wholly and entirely to Mary, and like Esau, he does not obey her in all things. False devotees of Mary include the following, namely:

Critical Devotees: They are known to be very proud and spiritually self sufficient. They pretend to be devoted to our heavenly Lady but in truth, they go about criticizing all true devotions made to her with humility, docility and tenderness by her children and servants, just because such devotions do not go in line with their own liking or because they do not understand them. They doubt foolishly all the miracles and pious stories recorded about Mary, and even regard them as exaggeration. They hate and grumble to see humble people praying before the *"IMAGE"* or *"GROTTO"* of the Empress of Heaven or even carrying her statue in rosary procession. And because they are spiritually blind, they argue that such devotion is idolatry and that what matters is for one to worship God in spirit and in truth. These people are very common in the church today.

Scrupulous Devotees: These include all those who have bluntly refused to honour Mary accordingly, in fear not to dishonour Jesus Christ her Son. They are highly envious and they argue that very little should be spoken of Mary, on the grounds that since Jesus is the one and only Saviour of mankind, Mary's role in the work of salvation is less important. They also argue that more people should pray before the Blessed Sacrament than before the Altar or Grotto of the Blessed Virgin as if the two, Jesus and Mary, are separable or as if those praying to Mary are not praying to Jesus through her.

The scrupulous devotees believe that Jesus should be preached all alone since he alone is our Saviour, but in truth, they only want to restructure, ridicule and hinder devotions to Mary. They say that Virgin Mary the Mother cast a shadow on the glory and the honour which is due to her Son alone. How senseless and how blind they are. How has the devil known how to capture them. They have reached such blindness because they neither listened to Jesus nor to his Mother, Mary. Like the critical devotees, scrupulous devotees are very common in the church today. They appear so holy and so catholic on the surface, but right in their hearts, they are Pentecostals within the church. They are very selective in the teachings and practices of the church. Their mode of worship is purely un-catholic and they see themselves as being possessed by the Holy Spirit, whereas they are tools in the hand of Satan, or Lucifer or the red dragon. They constitute most of the problems the church is facing today. They are very antagonistic in their relationship with the church, and their utmost aim is to destroy the church and our Blessed Mother, in pretext that they want to renew the church. By their fruit you will know them *Lk. 6:43-45; Mt. 7: 15-20; Mt. 12:33-35.* Children of God, be careful that these people do not confuse you.

External Devotees: These ones are fond of making all sorts of external devotions, but in truth, they have no interior love for Mary. They may say heavy quantities of rosary, enroll in all Marian societies in the church, hear many Masses yet cannot amend their lives and learn to imitate the virtues of the Holy Virgin. External devotees are the most critical of all false devotees.

Presumptuous Devotees: They include all those who are devoted to our Blessed Mother but have bluntly refused to amend their sinful lives under the pretext that they are devoted to her. They presume that since they say their rosaries, fast on Wednesdays and Fridays, belong to one Marian society or the other, wear the scapular or the little chain, their salvation is guaranteed. They believe that since they are devoted to the Holy Mother of Mercy, they cannot die without confession. They rely greatly on stories about how some great sinners obtained contrition at the moment of their death due to some devotions they practiced to Mary in their life time, to obtain similar favours.

Hypocritical Devotees: These ones are fond of covering their sinful habits with the mantle or scapular of Our Lady, in order to be taken by people for what they are not.

Interested Devotees: They include all those who invoke the gracious Lady, only to achieve their selfish interests. They are fond of running to her only to obtain one favour or the other, or to avert one danger or the other without which they would abandon her altogether.

In summary, all false devotees of Mary should be greatly feared and avoided. For they are very successful in contaminating people's true faith and depriving them of their true devotion to Mary, in pretext that they want to prevent its abuses.

Finally, children of God, now that you have known what makes a person a true or false devotee of Mary Mother of God, the question is, who am I, a true or false devotee? If I am a false devotee, what am I supposed to do to become a true devotee? But if I am a true devotee, what am I supposed to do in order to consolidate? Answers to all these questions have been carefully and lovingly given to you. The choice is yours.

C H A P T E R 2 0

MARY
OUR MEDIATRIX

The term Mediatrix should be understood in the context of Christ's desire that all believers should be mediators. A mediator is one who stands in the middle of two or more persons acting on behalf of the weaker party, in relation to the stronger. A mediator or intercessor brings people together, and Christ certainly wants every believer to bring others to him as Andrew brought Peter to him and as Philip brought Nathaniel *Jn. 1: 40-51*. We are all called to be coworkers with Christ, that is, to share in his saving work. When Saint Paul said, *"In my flesh I am completing what is lacking in Christ's sufferings on behalf of his body, that is, the church"* *Col. 1 : 24*, he was describing how he, and all believers, share in the saving work of Christ. Since all believers should be mediators and coworkers with Christ, we are surely being faithful to the Bible and to Christ when we call Mary our Mediatrix.

Some people argue that since *"there is one mediator of God and man, the man Christ Jesus" - 1 Tim. 2 : 5,* there is no need praying to God through Mary, Angels or Saints. They hold that praying to God by any means other than Christ results in idolatry. They forget that the same Saint Paul who wrote those words in his letter to Timothy, on another occasion, referred to Moses also as a mediator or a go-between - *Gal. 3 : 19.*

In calling the Blessed Virgin Mary our Mediatrix, either of the following facts should be taken into consideration, namely:

a. *Because, as worthy mother of God and full of grace, she occupies a middle position between God and His creatures.*

b. *Because, together with Christ and under Him, she cooperated in the reconciliation of God and humankind while she was still on earth.*

c. *Because she distributes the graces that God bestows on His children, you and me.*

When we call Mary our Mediatrix or Dispenser of all graces, we mean that all favours and blessings granted to us by God are granted in virtue of Mary and by her intervention. In this situation, Mary's action has a universal dimension; it involves all celestial and human beings with the sole exception of Jesus Christ and Mary herself. Because those whose existence preceded Mary's temporal existence (e.g. the Angels, Adam and Eve etc) received all their graces in view of her future merits and intercession which were, of course, present to God from all eternity, and indeed with a logical priority to their predestination. It involves also every supernatural favour *(sanctifying and actual grace)* and even blessings of the temporal order bearing some relation to the supernatural order.

Children of God, we are not saying that Mary is the producer of the sanctifying grace we receive through the Sacraments. Rather, she is involved in it in the sense that the actual grace we need to receive the Sacraments worthily is given to us because of her intervention. Hence the church refers to her as the *"channel"*, *"aqueduct"*, or *"treasurer"* of Divine grace. These are not to be understood in a literal sense, as if the Blessed Virgin were the physical instrument of grace. She is not. The manner in which she exercises her role is, specifically, by way of intercession. Whether we believe this or not, the truth is that whatever we receive from God passes through her. Mary is our loving Mother in the supernatural realm. She knows our needs and wishes to help us in all of them. She has that motherly intuition that just by mere looking at her Image is enough for her to know what our problems are, and she moves straight away to get solution to them. And since she is the mother of God, her prayers on our behalf cannot but be most powerful and efficacious. There is nothing

God cannot grant her. In the book of *Song of Songs 4 : 11*, the Bible testifies to this: *"The taste of honey is on your lips, O my spouse; your tongue is milk and honey for me. Your garment has the fragrance of Lebanon."*

The beauty, power and perfection of Mary's prayers have made the Holy Spirit describe them as honey and milk thereby making us to understand that Mary's prayers and requests are most efficacious or irresistible so to say, before the throne of God. We should always pray to her. We should not deny her the glory of obtaining favours for us, from God.

The mediation of Mary, Angels and Saints does not take away or add anything to the dignity and efficacy of Christ the one Mediator. Rather, it implies sharing in his saving work. In agreement with this view the Second Vatican Council says: *"The unique mediation of the Redeemer does not exclude but rather gives rise among creatures to a manifold cooperation that is but a sharing in this unique source"* (LG 62). Indeed the Angels, the Saints and the Priests of the New Testament can all be regarded as mediators between God and man in a true, though secondary, sense. The following Biblical passages attest to what we have so far discussed in this section, namely:

Revelation 8 : 3 - 4. Here an Angel of the Lord receives prayers from God's people on earth and offers them to God on their behalf. This way, angels are confirmed as *"Intercessors"* between God and man.

2Maccabees15 : 12 - 14. Jeremiah the great prophet, having died and gone to heaven, appears here as a Saint, praying and interceding for all God's people on earth.

Revelation 5 : 8. Angels and twenty four (24) Jewish Elders (Saints) appear to be receiving prayers from God's people on earth (i.e. you and I) and offering them to God.

Hebrews 13 : 18 - 19. St. Paul requests the Hebrews to pray for him and his colleagues that they may complete their work of evangelization. Thus, if people on earth can pray for one another and God answers them, why can't Mary, Angels and Saints who are always face to face with God, pray for us?

Exodus 32:13-14. Moses beckons on the Saints (Abraham, Isaac and Jacob) to save his people from divine punishment.

Daniel 10: 13; 11: 1 and *12: 1.* Angel Michael guards and prays for the people of God. The name Michael means *"who is like God?"*

Tobit 12: 12 -18. Archangel Raphael protects the family of Tobit, cured Tobit, and offered their prayers to God.

Exodus 23 : 20 - 22. God Himself confirms the teaching about guardian angels and the need we have of them. He tells us that these angels are meant to guard, defend and lead us always and that we must cooperate with them by being humble, attentive, obedient, and docile to them. He even says He will fight for us against the enemy if we can keep to this instruction, but quickly warns against disregarding the order. See also *Ps. 91: 11-12*.

Genesis 19 : 1-2. Here Lot saw two angels of the Lord coming to destroy Sodom; he got up and went to meet them. He revered them, prostrated on the ground and worshipped God. The Bible uses this event to explain to all and sundry that Angels must be revered and obeyed by men as this has been the will of God.

Philemon 5 - 7. Here Saint Paul praises Philemon for his strong love and faith, with regard to his devotion to the Saints. He then urges everyone to emulate him. He concludes that this is a genuine way of showing practical and effective faith in the Lord Jesus Christ.

Finally, we should note that the Bible uses the word *"Saints"* in two contexts, namely: those *(earthly)* who believe in Jesus Christ *Mt. 27 : 52 ; Rm. 1:7* etc, and all those who have really attained union with Christ in heaven *Col. 3: 4* and *Rev. 7: 14 17*. These are the ones we greatly request their prayers and intercessions. It is very important to note that apart from praying to God through Mary, we can also pray through Angels and Saints because their spiritual merits, qualities and attributes have made them greater in dignity, familiar, and in greater association with God and greater in the splendour of divine grace. They are perfectly righteous in the presence of God and the prayers of righteous men have powerful merits *James 5:16* and *Prov. 15: 8*. And since they act on behalf of the weaker party in relation to the stronger, we as the weaker party in relation to God should embrace them and seek their prayers and intercessions.

C H A P T E R   2 1

MARY
THE WOMAN PREFIGURED BY JUDITH

I n the Old Testament, Nebuchadnezzar who was the king of Babylonia, had conquered several nations of the world and destroyed their *idols*, and ordered that all should worship him and pray to him as a *god*. He threatened to destroy any nation which refused to adhere to his command. At that time, every nation except the Jewish nation accepted to adhere to this order. The Jewish people said that they would not worship any god other than the one and the only true God. As a result, Nebuchadnezzar became furious and declared them his greatest enemy. He vowed to fight and wipe the Jewish nation out of the face of the earth. At that time, *Holofernes* was the general in command of Nebuchadnezzar's armies and second in command to the king *Judith 2:4*. He was a Great War leader and the most feared by all nations.

When the Israelites heard what Holoferness had done to

other nations; how he had looted and destroyed all their temples, they were terrified of him and afraid of what he might do to Jerusalem and to the Temple of the Lord their God. They had only recently returned home to Judah from exile and had just rededicated the Temple and its altar after they had been defiled *Judith 4: 1-3*. So they prepared for war. They fasted and prayed earnestly to God to help them. God heard their prayers and saw their distress. To rescue them from the enemy, God sent them a Jewish widow who was deeply religious. The widow's name was *Judith*. Judith was such a beautiful woman that she attracted the attention of any man who saw her. No man had ever passed her without saying one good thing or the other about her irresistible beauty. She was full of holiness and compassion. She had great love for the Jewish people and was very prayerful. She was a woman of great virtues. God had adorned her with wonderful wisdom.

In the battle against *Holofernes* and his army; the enemy of God's own people, Judith's weapon was made up of her beauty, prayers, faith and all other virtues with which she had been adorned by God. Making use of all these, she quietly entered the camp of Holofernes and was invited to stay with him in his room. She made Holofernes to drink to stupor. And when it became obvious that he had been seized by alcohol, he felt asleep. At this juncture, Judith moved straight - away to him, seized him by the hair of his head and chopped off his head with the sword *Judith 12 : 10 - 20; 13 : 4-10.*

The next morning the Israelites, on the advice of Judith, hung the head of *Holofernes* on the wall of the town and there was panic in the camp of *Holofernes Judith 14: 11-19*. As a result, the soldiers scattered in different directions from the camp, running away for their dear lives. The Israelite soldiers took advantage of this and came charging down on them. In the end, the enemies were captured and conquered. This was how God used a woman to rescue his own people *Judith 15: 1- 7*. This event gives significance to the passage of the Bible that says, *"God purposely chose what the world considers weak in order to shame the powerful"* - *1 Cor. 1:27*.

Beloved children of God, in this mysterious battle, Judith was a *"Prefigure"* of the Blessed Virgin Mary, the woman whom God has chosen from all eternity and has superabundantly empowered her, and assigned her the task of going into spiritual battle with Satan. On the other hand, Holofernes who was the enemy of God's own people in the Old Testament, was a *"Prefigure"* of Satan who himself is the real enemy of God's own people in the New Testament the Christians the Israelites of the New Testament the true sons and daughters of Mary in *Rev. 12:17*.

Just like Judith, Mary is full of love and compassion for all children of God. And her weapon is also made up of her beauty, but in an extra ordinary manner. Hence the Bible speaks in praise of her: *"How pretty you are, how beautiful; how complete and graceful you are"* - *Song of Songs 7: 6 - 7*.

Mary's beauty includes purity, chastity, holiness, humility, prayer, obedience, wisdom, faith and all other virtues with which she has been adorned by God. All these put together form her weapon, and this weapon is more powerful and sophisticated than that of Judith because Mary alone is full of grace. Making use of this weapon, Mary confidently seized Satan by his head and crushed him to pieces *Gen 3:15; Rev. 12: 13-17*. In other words, she kept the word of God in *excelsis* and brought forth into the world Jesus the Saviour and Redeemer of mankind. In this way, the human race has been restored to life. This is how God has used a woman to rescue his own people. The greatest lesson of this mysterious event (as it concerns Judith and Mary) is that, while Judith was used by God to conquer Holofernes and chop off his head, in order to rescue his people in the Old Testament, Mary is the instrument used by God to conquer Satan, the implacable enemy of the human race and crush his head to pieces, in order to rescue his people forever from his dominion in the New Testament.

Now having conquered Holofernes and rescued the Jewish nation, Judith was honoured and blessed by the people. At the occasion, one of the town officials called *Uzziah* spoke on behalf of the people and said to Judith: *"O daughter, the Most High God has greatly blessed you more than all women on earth. Blessed be the Lord, who made heaven and earth because he has given you great power with which you cut off the head of our deadliest enemy. Blessed be his name for he has so magnified your name this day that your praise shall not depart out of the* mouth of men, and in every nation that shall hear your name, the Lord God of Israel shall be magnified because of you. May you be honoured and blessed forever"- Judith 13:18-20. After the people had finished showering praises on Judith, she was full of joy. She then offered thanksgiving to God by singing a song of praise to him, in gratitude and appreciation Judith 16:1-17.

Beloved brothers and sisters, my dear humble readers, the Blessed Virgin Mary is the woman in whom all these things are fulfilled. She alone is the daughter of the Most High God and the woman blessed more than all women Lk. 1: 42, because Jesus Christ is the fruit of her womb. Because of this great thing which the Lord has done for her Lk. 1:49, Mary's soul magnifies the Lord and her spirit rejoices in God her Saviour Lk. 1: 46-47. This offering of thanksgiving to God by Mary, in gratitude and appreciation, is what the Bible refers to as Mary's *Song of Praise* or the *Magnificat* of Mary Lk. 1: 46-55. Hence her praise shall never depart out of the mouth of men, that is to say, all generation shall call her blessed *Prov. 31: 31; Lk. 1: 48*. And in every nation that shall hear her name, the Lord God of Israel, shall be glorified because of her. Yes, because by means of Mary, He has redeemed the whole of humanity and recovered his image and likeness which had been seized by Satan, the deadliest enemy of his own people.

In celebrating the victory brought to them by Judith, the Israelite people came together. The High Priest Joachim and the Council of Israel came from Jerusalem. They honoured and praised Judith. In the end, they said to her, *"You are Jerusalem's crowning glory, the heroine of Israel, the pride and joy of our people" Judith 15:9.* In the same way, after Mary had successfully done the work God assigned to her on earth and won victory for him and all his people, she was celebrated in heaven. And when she died and was assumed (or carried) body and soul into heaven, she was honoured and praised by God. And for her reward, the Most Holy Trinity crowned her the glorious Queen of Heaven and earth, and proclaimed her the *Crowning Glory* of the New Jerusalem, the *Heroine* of the New Israel, the *Pride* and *Joy* of God's own people *Ps. 45 : 9; Rev. 12 : 1.*

Finally, what Judith of the Old Testament could only signify, Mary makes a reality and in a personal way; she is an effective sign of God's victory with his chosen people the Israelites of the New Testament the Catholic Church. And just as no one dared to threaten the people of the Old Israel, as long as Judith lived, so also, in all truth, no one will ever dare to threaten the Catholic Church and her faithful children, not even Satan, as long as the Most Powerful Virgin lives, and that is, forever. Oh, she is the true Heroine of the New Israel (or the Catholic Church), and the Pride and Joy of our race.

May all generation thank God very immensely now and forever for this good and wonderful Mother, who was promised us immaculate, conceived immaculate, born immaculate, lived and accomplished her task immaculate, died immaculate, resurrected and was taken into heaven body and soul immaculate, and is now reigning as Noble Queen of Heaven and earth immaculate.

REFERENCES

1. **The Bible** Douay Version / New Jerusalem

2. **The Glories of Mary** St. Alphonsus De Liguori

3. **True Devotion to Mary** St. Louis Marie De Montfort

4. **The Imitation of Mary** Alexander De Rouville

5. **The Mystical City of God** Mary of Agreda

6. **A Catholic Guide to Mary** Oscar L.

7. **Dictionary of Mary** Cath. Book Comp.

8. **The New Concise Catholic Dictionary**
    Reynolds R.E.

9. **The life of Jesus Christ and Biblical Revelations**
    Catherine Emerich

DEAR HUMBLE READERS

"No one lights a lamp and covers it with a bowl or puts it under a bed. Instead, he puts it on the lampstand, so that people will see the light as they come in" Mk. 4 : 21; Lk. 8 : 16. Thus, this knowledge which the Lord has given to me as a *"Lamp"* is now being put on the lampstand by means of this publication. It will always give you light for you to see as you make your journey on these days of darkness, filled with false doctrine, apostasy and fake theology.

Please, as this book reaches you, the same obligation falls on your shoulder to spread the knowledge to others. That is to say, you must always put the lamp on the lampstand for people to see the light. You can buy as many books as possible and distribute to people as gifts. You can even give them to people as *Souvenirs* at various occasions. I tell you, you will be drawing souls to Jesus through Mary. Congratulations then to you whose eyes the Lord has opened Mt. 11 : 25.

Brethren, let us always be meek and humble so that we can learn from Jesus. For it is only the humble who can accept to seek their salvation from God as sons and daughters of the Blessed Virgin Mary *(BVM)*, whereas the proud will always rely on their own strength alone to reach God, and like Esau, will have no regard for Mary as they continue to reject and attack her. Then on the judgment day, these same people will stand to tell Jesus that in his name, they proclaimed God's message, drove out demons, and performed many miracles and wonders. And if you (the reader) were Jesus Christ the Son of Mary, will you receive them? The answer to this question is emphatic no. For Jesus will quickly turn his back on them and say: *"I never knew you or what you are talking about. What message did you proclaim? God's message without Mary, Mother of God? Do you not know that the Good News you claim to have proclaimed started with Mary? And that the Jesus, in whose name, you claim to have performed miracles and wonders remains an inseparable and obedient Son of Mary? Have you forgotten that you all have sinned and fallen short of my grace, together with your first mother, Eve Rm. 3:23; 1 Jn. 1: 8-10, and you needed a second mother who has no sin in herself, and is full of my grace, to bring you back to me? She is no person other than my own worthy mother. She alone is full of my grace Lk. 1: 28. Today, you hear people claiming to have seen and received the light yet these same people reject my mother. How can somebody claim to have received the light whose source he constantly rejects? I am the light, and since I came into the world by means of Mary, she is the source.*

Light and its source are inseparable. Whoever rejects my Mother also rejects me the Son, and whoever rejects the Son also rejects the Father 1Jn. 2: 23. Have you forgotten that I am a faultless God and that whatever I do is faultless? How then, could you fault your God by rejecting his chosen Mother? How can you reject my Mother who is also My Queen and think you can have me the King? Don't you know that the King and his Queen are inseparable although you enviously and unrepentantly separated us on earth? How can you cast aspersions on my Mother and I welcome you? How can you speak against my own dear Mother, then claim to love Me and I receive you? Is there anyone whose friend would speak and fight against the mother, then claim to love him, and he welcomes the person? Of course no. Did I not say that whoever that loves Me should prove his love by keeping my commandment? Jn. 14:15. How then do you claim to love me yet you disobey my very own commandment? The last commandment I gave to humanity on earth was to accept Mary as their own true mother (of which she is), to honour and obey her in everything, and above all, to love her with all their hearts: "Son, behold your mother" Jn. 19 : 27. But this very commandment, you have rejected and ridiculed. And since the failure to keep one commandment means the failure to keep all others, you have failed in all of the commandments. Therefore, go away from us, you envious and unrepentant wicked people" Mt. 7: 21 - 23; Lk. 13: 25 - 27.

Children of God, having gone through this book, and having discovered and acknowledged the vital position of the Virgin Mary as it concerns your salvation, the question now is, is my *"faith"* Marian enough as intended by God? Am I then so committed? Please, accept the truth as contained in this book. Do not delay to do so, for delayed obedience is disobedience. Do not be deceived by those learned, proud false teachers, who would attack this message with insults because they do not understand it *2 Pt. 2 : 12.* The Lord has hidden it from them and revealed it to *you. Today that you have heard God's voice harden not your hearts Ps. 95: 7 - 8.* At this juncture I say with Jesus: *"Father, I have given your message to the world" Jn. 17:14.*

Beloved humble readers, if you appreciate this work (i.e. the book in your hand now) which our Most Gracious Mother has done through me, her unworthy servant, kindly recommend me to her protection and glorious intercession. Wherever I am, I will be doing the same thing for you. You can also write to tell me what you have learnt from this publication, what you now feel about Mary in your salvation and in fact, in the salvation of the whole of humanity. Once again, I urge you to always put this lamp which the Lord has given to you on the lampstand for people to see the light. May God bless you and nourish your souls as you join his Mother Mary, in the battle to crush the head of Satan to pieces. May you always remain in the peace of the Lord. And may we all meet in heaven by means of Mary, the Gate of heaven, amen.

I thank you, merciful Jesus, for having revealed this knowledge to me. With Virgin Mary, your dear and inseparable mother, I say to you: *"My soul magnifies the Lord; and my spirit rejoices in God my Saviour, for he that is mighty has done great things for me and holy is his name,"* Amen.

TESTIMONIES

1.This book contains careful selection from the Bible, where Mary Mother of God played a wonderful role in our salvation. It discloses and solves some problems in our faith. I am sincerely praying that entire mankind, endeavour to emulate and comply with it. In fact, I heaved a sigh of relief after going through the booklet. It is a great weapon which I believe, God in his infinite mercy, has given to mankind, to fight against Satan and heretics.

> *Vincent De Paul Mobi*
> *Ex Philosopher of Education,*
> *Bigard Memorial Seminary, Enugu.*

2.It is with deep regards that I commend the author's untiring efforts towards re-awakening the entire Christendom. This commendation is due to his ignorance therapy text *"Mary in the Bible"*.

Reading through this applauded text, I had the conclusion that the world staggers religiously due to ignorance. This, though prophesied in the Bible *Hosea 4: 6*, has thrown much dust in our eyes. Thanks to God that He maintains his word of *Heb. 13:8*, making our Priests and laity like GregMary spiritually alert. May He continue to inspire and bless him for more work ahead.

> *Bro. Henry Uzoma*

3.This book is truly inspired by the Holy Spirit of God. We (staff and students) have read it and wish to express that it is supposed to be in the hands of every Catholic. It should also be given to our non-Catholics and Contemporaries as gifts. It really brings out the hidden truth about our mother Mary in the Bible. The book is a treasure. One should not miss it. We are grateful to God for having given us such a wonderful book of testimony through his humble servant, Greg-Mary. This is a book for the time.

On the 1st of March, 2001, we invited the author to speak to us on the roles of Mary in the economy of salvation. The talk began at 8. 10am on the dot. While our speaker was talking, all of a sudden, his whole body transfigured into dazzling light, emitting colours of different kinds. Then, there was a stupendous miracle or dancing of the Sun that lasted for 30 minutes. This miracle began at about 9.00am. As the Sun spinned and danced, the Blessed Virgin suddenly appeared in the sky, smiling and waving to everyone. At a point, the Sun seemed to have changed into a large host and was no longer sharp to the eyes: that people could look at it without pains. The Sun emitted colours of different kinds: changing from white to yellow, to red, to golden, and finally to blue. In the end, it became encircled by a very beautiful rainbow. The entire school environment was turned into blue colouration, to the amazement and admiration of everyone, both Catholics and non-Catholics, everyone wanting to touch our august visitor, *Greg-Mary*. There was a great change in the atmosphere: the weather was very quiet. It seemed as if it was going to rain. There was a gentle breeze, even as blessed dew poured down from heaven upon everyone. We all rejoiced, jubilated, sang the praises of Mary, danced for her, and waved to her, to the Sun. In the end, the Queen of heaven blessed everyone and disappeared into heaven. This was how the heavens testified to the good work of Greg. This was how God and Mary honoured and glorified him. Please, may we all listen to him.

    Catholic Staff and Students,
    Metu Memorial Sec. School,
    Odoakpu Onitsha, Anambra State.

"As I have given my Rosary to you, mankind, through St. Dominic, and my Scapular through St. Simon Stock, I also give you another great weapon, "Mary in the Bible", through my child, GregMary that you may learn more about my holy Mother and Myself. Do not make mockery of it. It will help you defend your faith, and win back to me, sinners and gone astray".

(Jesus Christ, 6th April, 2001, at a public apparition, Maryland, Obowo, Imo, State)

"This book 'Mary in the Bible' is the fig tree of God whose leaves will scatter and spread in the air. It has already started spreading in the air. Pray more towards this and watch out for the war that will come as a result of this book. Pray hard and fear not. For I, the Great Warrior (Dike) will always protect you, my child. Pray for those who will make mockery of this book".

(Agonizing Jesus Christ to GregMary, 24th January, 2008, through the Stigmatist and Mystic, Sr. Uche Ojukwu, 38 Nanka, New Haven, Enugu)

CONTACT
GregMary Emeka Ajide

(Unworthy Servant of Jesus and Mary)
St. Gabriel's Catholic Parish,
Box 30, Ifitedunu, D.L.G.A.
Anambra State.
            OR

GregMary Emeka Ajide

Virgo Clemens International (VCI)
(Marian Centre and Apostolate)
Enugu State
Phone: +2348033817174
        +2347082489926

Email: celinamary@mariansociety.org
Other Books Written By The Author
- Mary's Tears (The reason why she cries)
- The Virgin Israel (Return O, Israel)
- The School of Mary
- Assumption and Coronation
- In The Name of Mary
- Purgatory in the Bible
- The Use of Holy Images
- My Call

Great Marian Miracle with "Mary in the Bible".

A young girl of 8yrs., from Saint Bernard Catholic Church, Ndiegoro, in the Catholic Diocese of Aba, Abia State, was kidnapped and searched for. On the 3rd day a young lady (Ifeoma), a teacher in a pre school, from same parish was also kidnapped by the same ritualists and taken to a bush in Ogbor Hill where they have their camp.

When the time came for Ifeoma to be killed she heard a big voice that said to her, "The book Mary in the Bible which you have in your hand is my Holy Mother's book. Now place it on your chest and you will be delivered", Ifeoma obeyed and placed the book on her chest. At this juncture the kidnappers' slaughtering machine broke to pieces. The Chief Ritualist came out fuming and ordered for her release. Pointing to the book on her chest he warned his gangs never to bring anyone in relationship with the woman on the book.

The 8yrs. old girl ran to go with Ifeoma but the man at the gate said no. He brought out a SWORD to cut Ifeoma to pieces but the reverse was the case: the SWORD turned and cut off his very own head by the invisible hand of God. In the end Ifeoma was rescued, along with the 8yrs. old girl. The testimony was given in the Church, in the assembly of God's children. This is how God used the book "Mary in the Bible" to rescue his daughters.

This Marian Miracle occurred in the month of July, 2013, two months after the author (GregMary) had Marian Program in the same parish.

> From Ifeoma (the Kidnapped),
> St. Bernard Catholic Church,
> Ndiegoro, Aba, Abia State